Everything for Winter

A COLLECTION FROM GRYPHON HOUSE BOOKS

Everything for Winter

A Complete Activity Book for Teachers of Young Children

Edited by Kathy Charner

Illustrations by Joan Waites

ACTIVITIES FOR DECEMBER, JANUARY AND FEBRUARY

gryphon house
Beltsville, Maryland

Published by Gryphon House, Inc.
10726 Tucker Street, Beltsville, MD 20705

World Wide Web: http://www.ghbooks.com

Text Illustrations: Joan Waites

Library of Congress Cataloging-in-Publication Data

Everything for winter : a complete activity book for teachers of young
    children : activities for December, January, and February / edited
by Kathy Charner.
        p.   cm.
    "A collection from Gryphon House books."
    Includes bibliographical references and index.
    ISBN-13: 978-0-87659-186-4 (pbk.)
    1. Early childhood education--Activity programs.   2. Early
childhood education--Curricula.   3. Winter.   I. Charner, Kathy.
II. Title: Complete activity book for teachers of young children.
LB1139.35.A37E85   1997
372.21--DC21   97-21455
                                                         CIP

Gryphon House is a member of the Green Press Initiative, a nonprofit program dedicated to supporting publishers in their efforts to reduce their use of fiber-sourced forests. This book is made of 30% post-consumer waste. For further information, visit www.greenpressinitiative.org.

Winter
Table of Contents

January

February

Introduction

Ever wish you could have the advice and suggestions of early childhood experts at your fingertips? It's in this book. With expertise in language, science, math, art, circle and group time, music, transitions and much more, this book gives you just what you need when you need it, in an easy-to-use format. This book contains activities, ideas and suggestions from the following time-tested books:

500 Five Minute Games
Earthways
Hug a Tree
More Mudpies to Magnets
More Story S-t-r-e-t-c-h-e-r-s
Mudpies to Magnets
One Potato, Two Potato, Three Potato, Four
Preschool Art
Story S-t-r-e-t-c-h-e-r-s
The Complete Learning Center Book
The Giant Encyclopedia of Circle Time and Group Activities
The Giant Encyclopedia of Theme Activities for Children 2 to 5
The Instant Curriculum
The Learning Circle
The Outside Play and Learning Book
The Peaceful Classroom
ThemeStorming
Transition Time
Where Is Thumbkin?

Activities appropriate for children

This book is chock-full of activities that teachers have used successfully with children for years. Teachers enjoy the activities because they are appropriate for children and because they are easy to do. Children enjoy the activities because they are fun and filled with things to learn. Whether you teach younger children or older children, or children who have difficulty understanding science concepts or those who need just a little extra help mastering language skills, there is something for you in this book.

A complete plan

Use this book to plan a morning, a day, a week, a month of activities, a whole season, or, with all three books, a whole school year. There are both teacher-directed and child-directed activities in the book. So while most of the children are independently exploring activities, the teacher can work with one or a few children who have expressed an interest in a certain area or who need additional work in a specific area.

A monthly plan

As written, this book offers teachers a complete plan for three months. Use this book to develop a monthly plan for December, January and February, using the variety of activities presented, or open the book to any page when you need an activity to fill a morning, a few hours or just a few minutes. This book offers both possibilities. The short sentence or paragraph that introduces each activity often contains learning objectives, an additional help to teachers for planning.

Integrated curriculum

Although the activities are drawn from different books, most of the activities in each month are related to certain topics or themes, the thematic threads of each month. Other activities related to the season or month (or because they were too much fun to leave out of the book) are also included in each chapter.

The thematic threads for December are:
> Gifts and Giving
> Traveling with Families
> Hanukkah, Christmas and Kwanzaa

The thematic threads for January are:
> Snow and Cold Weather
> Doctors and Helping Others
> Warm Food

The thematic threads for February are:
> Nighttime and Sleeping
> Valentine's Day
> Red and Other Colors
> Transportation

Create your own integrated curriculum that meets the needs and interests of your children by selecting related activities for one day, such as circle time, art and math activities, or plan a whole week of activities about Gifts and Giving (or Snow and Cold Weather or Transportation or any other thematic thread) that includes activities from all areas of the curriculum.

The monthly chapters

This book has three chapters; each chapter is a complete month of activities containing the following:

Fingerplays, songs and poems—use them during circle time or enjoy them anytime during the day.

Ideas and suggestions for 2 learning centers—learning centers are great child-oriented places where children experiment, create and learn about their world.

Art activities—children love to express their thoughts, feelings, accomplishments and discoveries through art. The activities focus on the process of art, not the product.

Circle time and group activities—activities for the times when all your wonderful individual children are learning to be part of a larger group. These activities, as with most of the activities in the book, are related to the month or the thematic threads of the month.

Dramatic play activities—children need little encouragement in this area. Just set up these activities, and let the children play!

Language activities—language acquisition, prereading skills and expressive language are just a few of the language skills children learn with these activities.

Math activities—activities that are fun, easy-to-do and appropriate for young children. The activities build a conceptual base to help children understand beginning math concepts.

Music and movement activities—children love to sing and move. Activities include old favorites and suggestions to turn old favorites into new favorites. Additionally, unique activities to encourage children to get up, move around and learn what their bodies can do are included in this section.

Science activities—filled with hands-on activities to help children begin to answer the many "why" questions and learn science skills of estimation, scientific method, problem solving, cause and effect relationships and lots more.

Snack and cooking activities—children love cooking projects—experimenting with ingredients, then proudly serving the result to the other children. Activities range from simple recipes with a few ingredients to those requiring more time and ingredients. Children will love them all!

Transition activities—ever wonder how to get a child who is engrossed in sand play ready for snack? Or clean up before circle time? Or get a group of children to come inside after outdoor play? Or to settle down to hear a story? This section is filled with tried-and-true activities.

Games—enjoy a fun time with a few children or the whole group. Play a game to help children learn math skills, coordination, language skills, listening skills, kindness or cooperation.

Suggested books—filled with books children and teachers love that are related to the season or the thematic threads of the month.

Recommended records and tapes—filled with records or tapes of songs that children and teachers love and that are related to the season or the thematic threads of the month.

The activities in each chapter

The activities in each chapter (month) contain the following:

Title of activity and suggested age—The title and suggested age tell what the activity is about and the ages most likely to enjoy and learn from the activity.
Note: Individual teachers are the best judges of children in their care. The ages are meant as a suggestion only.

Short introduction—This short sentence or paragraph describes the activity, suggests a learning objective or a combination of both.

Words to use—Language skills and vocabulary acquisition are developing rapidly in young children. Use this list of words while doing the activity, when talking about what the children will do or when discussing the activity after completion. The words range from simple to complex. Individual teachers will know best which words to introduce and use with their children.

Materials—A list of all the materials needed for the activity.

What to do—A step-by-step description of each activity. Helpful hints are often included as well as any cautionary notes necessary.

Want to do more?—This section includes suggestions for extending the activity using different materials or expanding it into other areas of the curriculum. For example, an art activity might suggest a different material to use instead of paper, or a circle time activity might suggest a related science or math activity.

Teaching tips—This section may include specific ways to help children with the activity. For example, a suggestion to tape the paper to the table so it does not move while the child is drawing. Or it may contain suggestions to make the activity simpler for younger children or more complex for older ones. Additionally, this section also may include general tips about working with children such as helping children learn respect for others, reminding teachers that young children get over-stimulated easily and other tips of that nature.

Home connections—The connection of home and school is a critical one. Teachers are often looking for ways to help parents feel more connected with what goes on in school. This section contains suggestions of how an activity can be done at home with parents, which may help parents feel more connected to the school or child care facility and help them understand what their child does during the day.

Books to read and records and tapes—Suggestions of books, records and tapes that relate to the activity.

DECEMBER

Fingerplays, Poems and Songs

Twinkle, Twinkle

Twinkle, twinkle little star,
How I wonder what you are.
Up above the world so high,
Like a diamond in the sky.
Twinkle, twinkle little star,
How I wonder what you are.

★ ONE POTATO, TWO POTATO, THREE POTATO, FOUR

Star Light, Star Bright

Star light, star bright,
First star I've seen tonight.
Wish I may, wish I might
Have the wish I wish tonight.

★ ONE POTATO, TWO POTATO, THREE POTATO, FOUR

Little Jack Horner

Little Jack Horner sat in a corner
Eating his Christmas pie;
He put in his thumb and pulled out a plum
And said, "What a good boy am I!"

★ ONE POTATO, TWO POTATO, THREE POTATO, FOUR

Two Fine Gentlemen

Two fine gentlemen met in the lane. (hold
   thumbs up)
Bowed most politely and bowed again. (bend
   thumbs toward each other)
How do you do, how do you do,
And how do you do again. (move thumbs as if
   they were talking to one another)

★ 500 FIVE MINUTE GAMES

Jingle Bells

Dashing through the snow,
In a one-horse open sleigh.
O'er the fields we go,
Laughing all the way.

Bells on bobtail ring,
Making spirits bright.
What fun it is to ride and sing,
A sleighing song tonight.

Jingle bells, jingle bells,
Jingle all the way.
Oh, what fun it is to ride
In a one-horse open sleigh.

Jingle bells, jingle bells,
Jingle all the way.
Oh, what fun it is to ride
In a one-horse open sleigh.

★ WHERE IS THUMBKIN?

Hanukkah Song

O Hanukkah, O Hanukkah,
Come light the menorah.
Let's have a party,
We'll all dance the horah.
Gather 'round the table,
We'll give you a treat.
Dreidels to play with,
And latkes to eat.

And while we are playing,
The candles are burning low.
One for each night,
They shed a sweet light
To remind us of days long ago.
One for each night,
They shed a sweet light
To remind us of days long ago.

★ Where Is Thumbkin?

Christmas Is Coming

Christmas is coming,
The goose is getting fat.
Please put a penny
In the old man's hat.
Please put a penny
In the old man's hat.

If you don't have a penny,
A ha' penny will do,
If you don't have a ha' penny,
Then God bless you,
If you don't have a ha' penny,
Then God bless you.

★ Where Is Thumbkin?

My Dreidel

I have a little dreidel,
I made it out of clay;
And when it's dry and ready,
Then dreidel I shall play.
Oh dreidel, dreidel, dreidel,
I made it out of clay;

Oh dreidel, dreidel, dreidel,
Now dreidel I shall play.

It has a lovely body,
With legs so short and thin;
And when it is all tired,
It drops and then I win.

Oh dreidel, dreidel, dreidel,
With legs so short and thin;
And when it is all tired,
It drops and then I win.

My dreidel is always playful,
It loves to dance and spin;
A happy game of dreidel,
Come play, now let's begin.

Oh dreidel, dreidel, dreidel,
It loves to dance and spin;
Oh dreidel, dreidel, dreidel,
Come play, now let's begin.

★ Where Is Thumbkin?

We Wish You a Merry Christmas

We wish you a Merry Christmas,
We wish you a Merry Christmas,
We wish you a Merry Christmas,
And a Happy New Year.

Now bring us some figgy pudding,
Now bring us some figgy pudding,
Now bring us some figgy pudding,
And a cup of good cheer.

We won't go until we get some,
We won't go until we get some,
We won't go until we get some,
So bring it out here.

We wish you a Merry Christmas,
We wish you a Merry Christmas,
We wish you a Merry Christmas,
And a Happy New Year.

★ Where Is Thumbkin?

December Learning Centers

Writing Center

While children are playing in the Writing Center they learn:

1. To communicate their ideas in written form.
2. The importance of written communication.
3. To appreciate the writing of others.
4. About computers and how they can be used in writing.

Suggested props for the Writing Center

typewriter
wipe-off cards
magic slates
chalkboards
writing tools such as
   markers
   pencils
   chalk
   colored pencils
stamp pad and letters
neon glue
craft sticks
writing materials such as
   lined and unlined paper in varied sizes
   graph paper
   computer paper
   construction paper
   butcher paper
   small slate board
   newsprint

Curriculum Connections

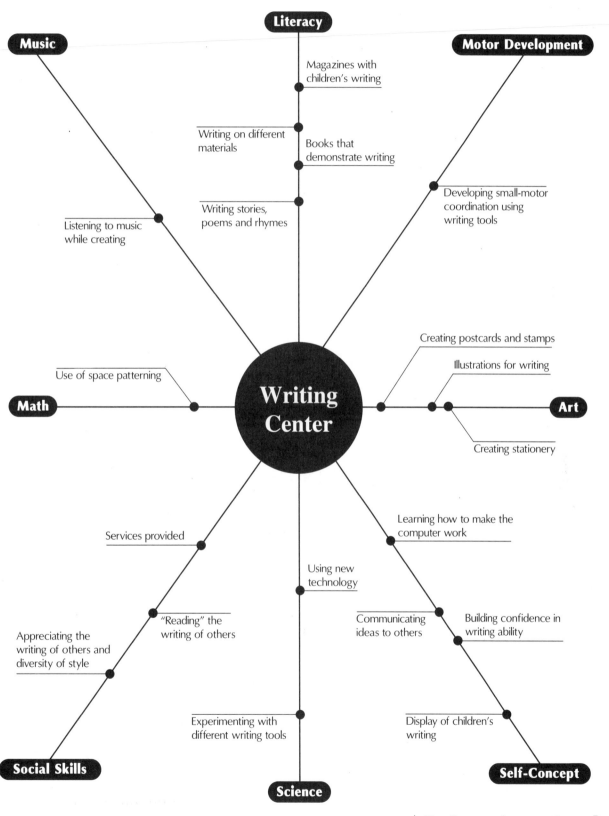

Music — Listening to music while creating

Literacy — Magazines with children's writing; Writing on different materials; Books that demonstrate writing; Writing stories, poems and rhymes

Motor Development — Developing small-motor coordination using writing tools

Math — Use of space patterning

Writing Center

Art — Creating postcards and stamps; Illustrations for writing; Creating stationery

Social Skills — Services provided; "Reading" the writing of others; Appreciating the writing of others and diversity of style

Science — Using new technology; Experimenting with different writing tools

Self-Concept — Learning how to make the computer work; Communicating ideas to others; Building confidence in writing ability; Display of children's writing

★ THE COMPLETE LEARNING CENTER BOOK

Toy Workshop Center

While children are playing in the Toy Workshop Center they learn:

1. To enjoy new books that relate to a specific theme.
2. To use the content of the stories in their play.
3. That they can create interesting toys that relate to the toy theme.
4. To improve their small motor coordination as they construct toys.

Suggested props for the Toy Workshop Center

books that relate to the center, such as
   The Moon Came Too by Nancy White Carlstrom
   Corduroy by Don Freeman
   Alexander and the Wind-up Mouse by Leo Lionni
   Play Day: A Book of Terse Verse by Bruce McMillan
   Things to Play With by Anne Rockwell
   Golden Bear by Ruth Young

old toys that can be repaired or decorated

stuffed animals including a teddy bear

sewing materials: large plastic needles, thick yarn, large buttons, fabric glue, trim, netting, an assortment of fabrics that are easy to sew, pieces of contact paper, hole punch, ribbons, cloth tape

repair box for fixing broken toys: screw driver, screws, electrical tape, contact paper, hammer, nails, clamp, glue

tempera paint and brushes

poster board and cardboard pieces

stickers and contact paper

plastic squeeze bottles

collection of balls

baby bath tub

junk items: plastic wheels, Styrofoam pieces, small bars of soap, straws, pieces of fabric, foil, toy catalogs, plastic trays, lids, refrigerator dishes, tin cans, buttons, pipe cleaners, etc.

Curriculum Connections

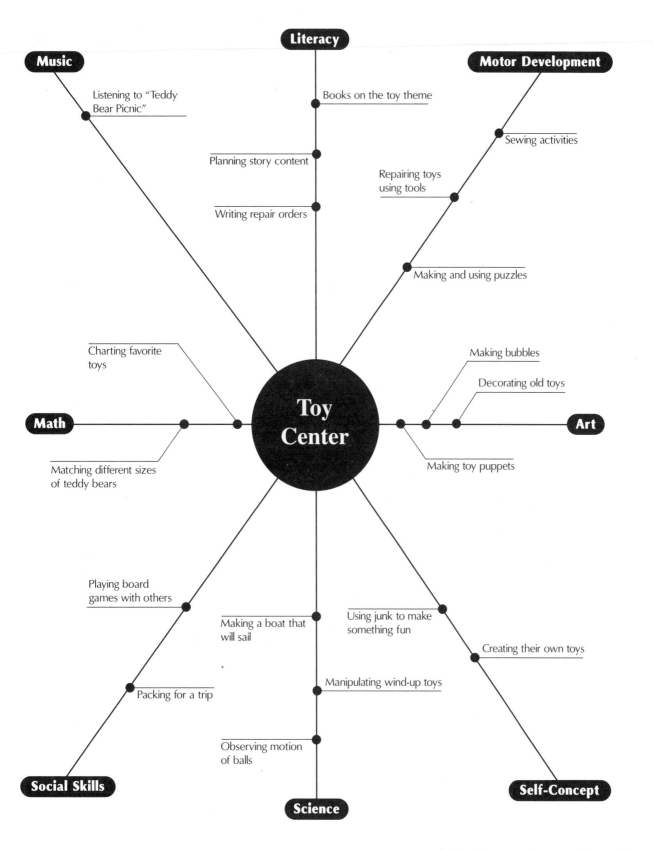

Music
Listening to "Teddy Bear Picnic"

Literacy
Books on the toy theme
Planning story content
Writing repair orders

Motor Development
Sewing activities
Repairing toys using tools
Making and using puzzles

Toy Center

Charting favorite toys

Math
Matching different sizes of teddy bears

Making bubbles
Decorating old toys
Art
Making toy puppets

Playing board games with others
Packing for a trip
Social Skills

Making a boat that will sail
Manipulating wind-up toys
Observing motion of balls
Science

Using junk to make something fun
Creating their own toys
Self-Concept

★ THE COMPLETE LEARNING CENTER BOOK

Art Activities

Pine Cone Bird Feeders

3+

This activity makes feeding winter birds enjoyable.

Words to use

bird
feed
pine cones
peanut butter
sticky
stick
snack

Materials

pine cones—long ones work best, but any kind will do
peanut butter—the cheapest sugarless kind you can find—many natural food stores allow you to buy
    it in bulk, so you can buy as much or as little as you want. Figure that you will be able to make
    approximately 10 pine cone bird feeders per pound of peanut butter.
popsicle or craft sticks or tongue depressors
bird seed—the least expensive kind you can find
cookie sheet or a pie plate to hold the seed
heavy string, twine or yarn
wax paper or wax paper bags

What to do

1. Apply the peanut butter to the pine cones with the craft sticks, pressing it into all the nooks and crannies. Expect that fingers will be licked and some peanut butter will be eaten. Just remind the children that this snack is really for the birds!
2. Roll the peanut butter-covered pine cones in the pan of bird seed. The bird seed will stick to the peanut butter. Gently shake off the excess.
3. Tie the string or yarn tightly around the base or top of each pine cone.
4. Perhaps the children could make two—one for school and one for home. This way you will have a supply to use at school and the children will be able to see how they attract the birds. Then the children will take them home enthusiastically!
5. Send them home in wax paper or wax paper sandwich bags. They are a lot less sticky than plastic (and more environmentally friendly).

★ EARTHWAYS

Fabric Transfer

Children learn about printing and how designs reverse when printed.

Words to use

design
draw
wax
iron
heat
transfer
reverse
print
fabric

Materials

fabric crayons
white paper
fabric—old sheet, muslin, a T-shirt or pillow case
old iron
pad of newspaper for ironing

What to do

1. Draw or color heavily with fabric crayons on white paper. (Follow the directions on the fabric crayon box.)
2. Place the fabric on the pad of newspaper.
3. Place the drawing face down on the fabric.
4. With adult help, press the paper with a warm iron using a firm straight ironing motion. Try not to peek or the picture may wiggle and blur. The picture from the fabric crayons will transfer to the fabric.
5. Remove the piece of paper with the fabric crayon design. The wax will have melted into the fabric and the heat will set the color into the fabric.

Want to do more?

Individual squares could be sewn into a quilt. Decorate a bandanna, book bag, cloth napkins, table cloth or any other fabric.

Teaching tips

Fabric crayons are available at all fabric and craft stores and often in art supply areas of stores that carry regular crayons. The drawings made with fabric crayons will not look like the drawings made with regular crayon but the transferred design will have bright and true colors. The colors may look different than regular crayons. Fabric crayon prints hold color well, even after repeated washing and drying.
Note: As with any ironing project, an adult should either do the ironing or supervise older artists with the ironing.

Wooden Candleholders

3+

Develops an appreciation for the beautiful materials in nature.

Words to use

pine cone
acorns
seed pods
bird seed

Materials

slices of logs—one per child—approximately 3-4 inches in diameter and 1 inch thick with a 3/4 inch hole drilled to a depth of 1/2 inch in the center of each slice

marker

non-toxic white or yellow glue—yellow carpenter's glue works very well

assortment of small things from nature: tiny pine cones (hemlock), acorns or acorn caps, tiny shells, sweet gum balls, small seed pods, nuts (especially filberts or hazelnuts) and cranberries (these provide a beautiful splash of color)—use anything that's not too large

bird seed and spoon, optional

What to do

1. Write each child's name on the underside of the candleholder.
2. Spread the glue, fairly thickly, all over the top of the candleholder, taking care not to get it in the hole that will hold the candle. The glue will dry clear.
3. The children choose natural objects and place them all over the top of the candleholders, pressing them down into the glue. Encourage the children to cover the top. If you want, you can sprinkle a spoonful of bird seed all over the top of the candleholder when the children have finished to fill in any spaces or holes.
4. Place the candleholder in an out-of-the-way place to dry.
5. If you are making candles—either dipping, rolling or decorating—wait until those are done and send one home in its own holder.

Note: Perhaps you can get a carpenter-parent or local woodworking shop to do the cutting and hole drilling for you. Take them your 3-4 inch diameter logs or branches and let them do the preparation on their equipment.

★ EARTHWAYS

Pomander Balls

These are fun to create and make great gifts.

Words to use

smell
holes
cloves
pomander ball

Materials

oranges, lemons or apples
push pins or small nails
whole cloves
spice mixture: ground cinnamon, allspice, cardamom, cloves—mix your own combinations
shallow pan to hold the spice mixture
yarn or ribbon for hanging

What to do

1. If necessary (when using a thick-skinned fruit), use the nail or push pin to puncture holes in the skin of the fruit about 1/4 inch apart.
Note: Supervise closely.
2. Press the whole cloves into the holes, or directly into the fruit, working to cover the entire skin of the fruit. This is a project which can be done over several days.
3. When the entire fruit is studded with cloves, roll the fruit in the spice mixture.
4. Knot two pieces of yarn or ribbon together at the middle and place the pomander over the knot. Take up the four ends, tie them together in a firm knot and then a pretty bow.
5. This project can be varied according to the age of the children. The five-year-olds should be able to do this by themselves. The three-year-olds may need the holes punched for them. Perhaps, rather than having each child make his or her own, the younger children can help with a "class pomander" to hang in the bathroom or in a sunny window.

★ EARTHWAYS

Pine Cone Fire Starters   3+

Children love making gifts that are useful like this one.

Words to use

wax
melt

Materials

wax—beeswax works fine but you may want to use the less expensive paraffin, or a mixture of both
old pan
pine cones—any kind will do, although the longer, thinner ones work best
yarn, ribbon or heavy thread
scissors
wax paper

What to do

1. Melt the wax in an old pan.
2. Tie a string or piece of yarn or ribbon around the wide end of each pine cone. Make a loop about four inches long at the end of the pine cone.
3. Holding the end of the string, dip the pine cone into the melted wax and slowly bring it out. Hold it above the can for a few seconds until it stops dripping. Repeat the dipping once or twice. Then lay the wax-covered pine cone on a piece of wax paper to harden.
4. Tie the string into a bow at the top, or tie three or four pine cones into a bundle. Keep them at school until gift giving time approaches. You can wrap them in tissue paper if you like. Include the following instructions with the fire starters:
   ✓ Instructions for Use: Place the pine cone fire starters in the fireplace and light them like kindling to start a fire.

★ EARTHWAYS

Glittering Pine Cones   3+

Make a beautiful tree ornament from natural items.

Words to use

pine cone
glitter
sprinkle

Materials

large pine cones (approximately 6″ long)
glue in a bottle
glitter in several different colors
box lid (to hold pine cones while glittering)
glue gun
red or green velvet ribbon

What to do

1. Gather the materials and place them on the table.
2. Have each child select a pine cone and hold it over the box lid.
3. The children squirt glue over the entire pine cone.
4. Have each child select color(s) of glitter and sprinkle over the pine cone.
5. Allow glitter to dry at least 24 hours.
6. Make a loop from the ribbon and use the glue gun to attach it to the bottom of the pine cone. Allow another 24 hours to dry to make sure the ribbon is secured to the pine cone.

Want to do more?

If children live in a section of the country where pine cones are plentiful, go on an outing so children can search for their own pine cones to decorate.

★ THE GIANT ENCYCLOPEDIA OF THEME ACTIVITIES

Decorating Windows with Snowflakes   3+

Children will learn to fold and cut snowflakes.

Words to use

snowflake
fold
cut

Materials

thin typing paper
scissors
tape

What to do

1. Show the children how to fold thin typing paper three times.
2. Demonstrate how to cut in and out at random, cutting notches and curves but leaving some of the edge uncut.
3. Unfold the paper to see the snowflakes.
4. Let the children tape their snowflakes to the windows.

Teaching tips

Invite a parent or grandparent who is an origami expert to come to class and demonstrate folding and cutting paper into animal and decorative shapes.

★ MORE STORY S-T-R-E-T-C-H-E-R-S

String Ornaments

3+

Sometimes string is soft and flexible and sometimes string is hard and rigid.

Words to use

string   glue
shape   glitter

Materials

various lengths of string or embroidery floss
white glue, thinned with water in a small bowl
wax paper
glitter
scissors
wet towel for clean up

What to do

1. Dip the string in the thinned glue.
2. Wipe excess glue off the string by pulling it through the pointer finger and thumb or by pulling it across the edge of the bowl. (Be ready to clean fingers with the wet towel.)
3. Place the string on the wax paper in any shape, design, pattern or form.
4. Sprinkle glitter over the string.
5. Dry the string design completely.
6. Gently peel the string design off of the wax paper.
7. Hang the string as an ornament if desired.

Want to do more?

Make definite shapes such as circles, stars, diamonds or other designs with the string. Add tempera paint to the thinned glue for a colored glue. Sprinkle other things on the ornaments such as colored sand, confetti or candy sprinkles.

Teaching tips

This project will need to dry at least overnight. Peeling the string from the wax paper can be tricky.

★ PRESCHOOL ART

Sponge Trees

Children express their creative abilities in this activity.

Words to use

sponge
tree
shape
dip

Materials

sponges cut into Christmas tree shapes
drawing paper
green tempera paint

What to do

1. Place the paint, sponges and paper out for the children to use.
2. The children dip the tree sponges in the green paint and create designs on their paper.
3. Older children can add details to the pictures when the paint is dry.

★ WHERE IS THUMBKIN?

Star Windows: Tissue Paper Transparencies

3+

This activity develops fine motor skills.

Words to use

star
window
transparent
stick

Materials

construction paper—deep red and blue
scissors
colored tissue paper—golds, yellows and white
basket or tray
pen
white glue, small saucers and cotton swabs (or pencils with new erasers) or glue sticks

What to do

1. Cut the construction paper into frames in the shape of your choice. A plain rectangle with rounded edges to soften the shape is fine; a star would be extra special, but will take longer to do. The total size is up to you, but make it no smaller than 6 inches long and 4 inches wide. The frame edge itself should be approximately 3/4 to one inch thick.

2. Run a bead of glue all around the back of the frame near the outer edge and press a large piece of white tissue paper over it. Trim the tissue paper.

3. Cut the yellow and gold tissue paper into star shapes, in varying sizes if you like. By folding the tissue accordion style, you can cut many stars at the same time. Place the stars in a basket or on a tray.

4. Write the children's names on the backs of the frames (the side with the tissue paper glued on). This is the side on which they work.

5. Give each child a glue stick or have them share a small dish or saucer of glue (just put a little on the dish). They could use a cotton swab to apply the glue, but use these sparingly as they cannot be reused. You can also use erasers on new pencils to dip in the glue and dab onto the stars. The erasers can be rinsed off and reused.

6. Using a tiny drop of glue for each star, the children cover the white tissue with stars. Encourage them to fill the surface, although the younger ones may just place a few stars on the tissue paper. It is fine to overlap the stars, as this creates interesting shapes and beautiful and surprising new colors.

7. When they have finished, add an extra covering of white tissue as you did in step two. While not completely necessary, it provides a nice protective backing and gives the transparency a more finished look.

8. Let the children hold them up to the light. The children are always captivated by the results.

9. Cover the classroom windows with star windows, or send each one home so the stars shine there. This technique for making tissue paper transparencies is endlessly variable. The frames can be cut into any shape, from pumpkins (fall) to eggs (spring). Just choose the tissue paper in seasonal colors and cut the construction paper into appropriate shapes. Generally, white tissue paper is used for backing in all cases.

★ EARTHWAYS

Light Holes

4+

Children learn fine motor skills while making a design with holes poked in the paper.

Words to use

poke
hole
cover
design
light

Materials

black paper
heavy cardboard for work surface
poking tools such as a pencil, nail, pin, bamboo skewer or scissors
tape
glue
scraps of colored tissue, cellophane and colored paper

What to do

1. Tape a square of black paper to the cardboard work surface.
2. Use the poking tools to punch holes in the black paper. Make as many holes in as many sizes as desired.
Note: See teaching tips.
3. Remove the tape.
4. Cover the holes with any colored paper by gluing or taping the papers on the back of the black paper. It is pretty to cover each hole or a few holes with small scraps of tissue or cellophane.
5. Place the Light Holes design in a window or hold it up to the light to see the colored lights.

Want to do more?

Make holes in a pattern or design. Work on black paper that has been cut into a pattern such as a tree, star or circle. Poke holes in colored paper and tape the paper to a sheet of black paper. The holes seem to "pop out" using this method. Glue the poked paper on a sheet of foil for shiny holes. Use a piece of plywood for the work surface and make all the holes using a hammer and nails.

Teaching tips

Note: When working with sharp tools supervise closely. Allow plenty of room between artists and set a rule that all sharp objects must be left on the table if the artist must get up for any reason. Some artists have not learned to control poking holes through paper. The paper can tear rather than making a hole. Paper tears can be taped on the back or may be incorporated into the final design.

★ PRESCHOOL ART

art activities

Stained Glass Melt

4+

Artists learn how to make drawings that look like stained glass windows.

Words to use

melted
outline
warming tray
stained glass

Materials

white paper
black felt pens
old crayons, peeled
warming tray
heavy glove or oven mitt
scissors and tape, optional

What to do

1. Use the black felt pen to outline a design on the white paper. The blank spaces will be "colored in" with melted crayon.
2. Place the paper with black outlines and drawings on the warming tray.
3. Put a heavy glove or oven mitt on the non-drawing hand. Hold the paper down with this hand.
4. Using the peeled crayons, color in the pen design. Working slowly will allow the crayon to melt and soak into the paper.
5. Remove the design from the warming tray. Hold the paper up to the light or a window and see the stained glass effect.
6. The design can be cut out and displayed in a window to resemble a stained glass window.

Want to do more?

Artists can observe real stained glass windows which will enhance their imaginations as they create. Rub the back of the crayon design with a cotton ball soaked in baby oil for a more transparent design.

Teaching tips

Note: As with any project involving heat or electricity, observe safety and caution. Tape the cord from the warming tray to the table and push the table against the wall. Some young artists will not have the concept of stained glass and will simply enjoy melting crayon in pretty but random experiments.

★ PRESCHOOL ART

Insole Stamps

Children learn how to make their own stamps.

Words to use

stamp
design
cut out
ink pad
print
shape
decorate
wrapping paper
greeting card

Materials

shoe insoles
pen
scissors
rubber cement or other glue
wooden block scrap
ink pad or paint spread on paper towels

What to do

1. Draw a design on the latex side (not the fabric side) of the insole.
2. Cut out the design with scissors.
3. Glue the cut-out shape to a scrap of wood with rubber cement or other glue.
4. When dry, press the block stamp into a regular ink pad. (If no ink pads are available, spread some paint or food coloring on a pad of paper towels in a Styrofoam tray and use like an ink pad.)

Want to do more?

The insole shape can be glued to a jar lid or a piece of heavy cardboard. Use this idea for decorating holiday wrapping paper or making greeting cards.

Teaching tips

Some young children tend to think that the harder they smash the stamp into the ink, the better the print will be. Encourage gentle but firm pressing for the best print ever. Other glues will also work if rubber cement is not available or if it is objectionable due to the odor or fumes it emits.

★ PRESCHOOL ART

Making Dreidels

4+

Children enjoy making this seasonal toy.

Words to use

dreidel
letters
spin

Materials

a 4" cardboard square
pencil

What to do

1. Draw a line on the cardboard square diagonally from one corner to the opposite one. Repeat for the other two corners.
2. Put dreidel letters G, H, S and N on each of the four resulting sections.
3. Poke a hole in the middle of the square large enough to fit a pencil snugly.
4. Poke a pencil into the hole to create a spinning top.
(See Dreidel Game and Activities, a circle time activity, on pages 41-42 for instructions on how to play a game with this dreidel.)

★ WHERE IS THUMBKIN?

Tissue Paper Dolls

4+

This method of making tissue paper dolls can be modified for many different occasions by using different colors. The children may want to make several dolls.

Words to use

head
stuffing
body
yarn

Materials

tissue paper—white or different colors
scissors
stuffing wool or cotton
string or strong thread
colored wool fleece and glue, optional

What to do

1. Cut tissue paper into two rectangles—one 4 x 8 inches and the other 3 x 6 inches. Use one color for both pieces or vary the colors.

2. Have the children form a bit of stuffing wool into a small tight ball about 1/2 inch in diameter. This will be the head.
3. Place the ball just about half way down the larger tissue paper rectangle and fold the tissue over it, gathering it where the neck should be.
4. Place the smaller tissue paper rectangle over the top of the head side to side and also gather this tissue paper around the neck, leaving the front open—this will be the face.
5. Help the children tie the thread (use it doubled if it's not strong) around the neck, knotting at the back of the head.
6. Twist the two ends of the smaller rectangle into arms and hands. The back will look like a small cape.
7. Fluff out the skirt so the figure will stand.

★ EARTHWAYS

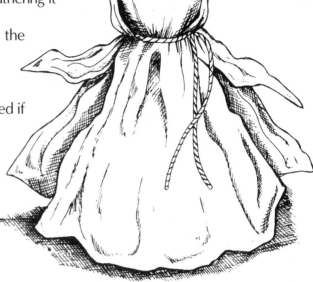

Yarn Dolls

4+

These little dolls are very easy to make. Children may need some help tying the knots.

Words to use

yarn
wrap
bundle

Materials

medium weight wool yarn in assorted colors (thinner yarn also works, but thick yarn is too bulky for this craft project)
scissors
firm cardboard, corrugated works best, cut into 3" x 5" pieces
fabric scraps, safety pins, optional

What to do

1. Measure out approximately 3 arm lengths (about 3 yards) of yarn and have the children roll it into a little ball. You will need one for each doll.
2. Give each child a piece of cardboard and a ball of yarn. Have them wrap all the yarn around the cardboard. Wind the yarn around the long way for a bigger doll (almost 5 inches tall) or around the width for a smaller doll.

3. Slide a short piece of yarn under the wrappings to gather them, and tie them tightly together.

4. Now slide the wrapped yarn off the cardboard. The tie will hold the yarn together.

5. Take a small piece of yarn and tie the bundle tightly where the neck should be. This creates the head.

6. Separate about 1/4 of the strands of yarn to the left and 1/4 to the right to form the arms (just do it by sight, it needn't be exact). Tie each of these smaller bundles where the wrist should be and trim away the excess. Don't make the arms too long.

7. Tie around the body bundle at the place where the waist should be. If you want to make a doll with a skirt, you can stop here. If you want to make a figure wearing pants, separate the body bundle into two bunches, tying each off at the ankle. Trim the ends.

8. Let the children help as much as possible with the knot tying. They can also help with the trimming.

9. The older children may wish to add clothes: scarves, shawls, belts.... This is a great way to use up felt and fabric scraps.

10. The 3 x 5 inch dolls make nice additions to the class toy collection and are useful when the children are building farms, villages, etc., to "people" their scenes. They may want to make several dolls. They are so simple that they leave lots of room for the imagination.

11. The smaller dolls also make sweet gifts as decorative pins. Just add a safety pin to the back, and you can pin them on hats, coats, etc.

← separate legs for pants

← attach felt and fabric scraps if desired.

← leave untied for skirt

★ EARTHWAYS

Window Paintings

Tired of painting on paper? Try the window!

Words to use

window
paint
sponge
wash
design
holiday scene
soap
clean up

Materials

paintbrushes
newspapers
tape
liquid tempera paints in containers
soapy water and sponge

What to do

1. Tape newspaper to the bottom edges of windows to protect floors and ledges.
2. Paint on the inside of the window so rain will not wash off the painting.
3. Leave the design on the window for days or weeks.
4. Wash the design off with a sponge and soapy water. (This is a messy job!)

Want to do more?

Paint holiday scenes or designs or use holiday colors to paint any designs. Cover the window with a large sheet of cellophane and paint on the cellophane instead of the window. Paint with white shoe polish and the applicators which come in the polish bottles. This is very easy to clean up. White is nice for snow scenes, too.

Teaching tips

Mix powdered tempera paint with liquid dishwashing soap and water for easier removal. Mix paint with white shoe polish for optional easy removal. The longer the paint is left on the window, the harder it is to remove.

★ PRESCHOOL ART

DECEMBER

art activities

Circle Time and Group Activities

Shining Stars

3+

Teaches appreciation of all the holidays of this season.

Words to use

excitement
holidays

Materials

yellow construction paper stars, large (1 per child)
yarn

What to do

1. Send a letter home to parents similar to the following sample letter. (After you have discussed the holiday season with the children, include their responses in the letter.)

> *Dear Parents,*
>
> *The holiday season is upon us! This means excitement is in the air. The boys and girls have expressed some of the changes this season brings in their homes. The children have talked about putting up a tree, hanging wreaths, lighting candles, watching a special show, baking cookies. Over the next few weeks, we will keep the routine fairly consistent, but we will talk about and do activities that relate to specific family traditions. Please take a few minutes to reflect on this season with your family and write down something your family does together that is a family tradition. Try to be specific in your description. Thank you for helping to make this season a unique and special one for the children.*

2. Make a large yellow construction paper star for each child. Punch a hole in one of the points.
3. Find a special spot in the room to hang each shining star as it is introduced.
4. Make a list of each child's family tradition as you receive it.
5. On one side of the star put the child's name. On the opposite side write the family tradition and illustrate the tradition with the child's help.
6. Laminate the stars and tie long pieces of yarn through the holes.
7. Each morning during circle time introduce one or more shining stars. (Consider the number of children in the class when planning the schedule so all the children will have a turn.) Ask the child to talk about the family tradition. During the day incorporate the tradition as a group experience, such as sending holiday cards, reading a story together, cooking or baking, making ornaments.

★ THE GIANT ENCYCLOPEDIA OF CIRCLE TIME AND GROUP ACTIVITIES

Little Drummer Girls and Boys   3+

Teaches children to identify one sound (a drum) and make an instrument that makes that sound.

Words to use

drum
story
music

Materials

Little Drummer Boy by Ezra Jack Keats
tin or cardboard cylinder boxes (coffee cans, oatmeal containers)
paper
glue
collage materials (Styrofoam peanuts, glitter, cotton, paper scraps)

What to do

1. At circle time read *Little Drummer Boy* and talk about sharing and the gift of music that the Little Drummer Boy gave.
2. Talk with the children about making drums and explain that each child will choose a container to make a drum.
3. Provide the materials, including paper, glue and collage items.
4. Wrap the paper around the container and decorate the drum.

Want to do more?

Field trip: Visit a nursing home and play the song while the children play their drums. Following the field trip, talk with the children about the responses they received to playing their drums. How did they feel sharing their drum playing with others.

Music: Play "The Little Drummer Boy" song and ask the children to play their drums when they hear the sounds "par-rum-pum-pum-pum."

★ THE GIANT ENCYCLOPEDIA OF CIRCLE TIME AND GROUP ACTIVITIES

Musical Christmas Present Surprise   3+

Teaches children patience and how to take turns.

Words to use

present
wrap
music
stop

Materials

8 to 10 boxes in graduated sizes (small to large)
small items for presents, such as children's rings, seasonal erasers
wrapping paper, ribbon and tape
recorded music

What to do

1. Wrap the present in the smallest box.
2. Put each box inside the next larger box, wrapping each box with wrapping paper and ribbon.
3. At circle time, pass the present around the circle as music is playing. When the music stops, the child holding the present opens it. Continue until the last present is opened.

★ THE GIANT ENCYCLOPEDIA OF CIRCLE TIME AND GROUP ACTIVITIES

Wonder Wands   4+

This activity encourages children to notice and appreciate what they think is beautiful around them.

Words to use

beauty
gentleness
appreciation

Materials

a dowel rod approximately 14" long for each child
decorative art materials (stars, glitter, ribbon, felt tip pens, etc.)
glue

What to do

1. Ask the children to describe what they think "beauty" means. Can they identify something they think is beautiful? Point out that people find different things to be beautiful. Provide a few examples of people who have different opinions about what is beautiful.
2. Show them a dowel rod. Tell them that they are going to decorate the rod to make pretend magic Wonder Wands. Describe the materials set out in the art area. "We can pretend that these Wonder Wands are like magic. We can gently touch something we think is beautiful with the wand and perhaps part of that beauty will become part of the Wonder Wand."
3. In the art area, work beside the children to make your own Wonder Wand.
4. When the wands are completed and the glue firmly dried, call the children together to show off their creations. Teach them the following poem to recite as they gently touch something they think is beautiful.

> *Here is a lovely thing;*
> *Of its wonder I will sing.*
> *My Wonder Wand will help me find*
> *A place for beauty in my mind.*

5. Touch something with the wand and repeat the chant. Then ask a child to do likewise. After several children have had a turn, encourage the entire group to explore the surrounding area with their Wonder Wands.
6. At the end of the school day, tell the children that they can take their Wonder Wands home. They can bring them back to school another day if they wish. Before dismissing the children, describe several things that you touched with your Wonder Wand and why you want to remember these things. Encourage children to identify what they touched.

Want to do more?

Consider touching each child in your class with the wand while reciting the poem. Read *Good Times on Grandfather Mountain* by Jacqueline B. Martin, illustrated by Susan Gaber (Orchard, 1992).

Home connection

Children can take their Wonder Wands home to show their parents. They also can teach their parents the poem and show them how to make wands.

★ THE PEACEFUL CLASSROOM

Dreidel Game and Activities   4+

Children love to play this seasonal game.

Words to use

dreidel
spin
game

Materials

plastic dreidel
peanuts

What to do

1. At circle time divide the children into groups of about five children each.
2. Each child counts out 20 peanuts.
3. Before each child takes a turn, the children each put one peanut in the middle of the group.

ה Hay ~ Take half

ג Gimel ~ Take all

נ Nun ~ Do nothing

ש Shin ~ Put one in

4. Each child in turn gets a chance to spin the dreidel. Depending on what Hebrew letter the dreidel lands on, the child must do the following: (see illustration)

HAY—*take half*
GIMEL—*take all*
NUN—*do nothing*
SHIN—*put one in*

If possible give each child a bag of peanuts, a plastic dreidel and directions on how to play the game to take home for a family gift.

Want to do more?

Art: Put paint on the tip of the dreidel and spin it on paper towels, or roll the dreidel in paint and then roll it on paper.
Cooking: Make dreidel cookies with a package of sugar cookie dough, dreidel shaped cookie cutters and sprinkles. Bake and eat.
Math: Ask the children to make a graph of the number of peanuts that each child has at the end of the game.

★ THE GIANT ENCYCLOPEDIA OF CIRCLE TIME AND GROUP ACTIVITIES

Light the Kwanzaa Candles   4+

This simple holiday season activity allows children to learn about an African cultural tradition. The harvest festival known as Kwanzaa is celebrated from December 26 until January 1st in many African-American communities.

Words to use

Kwanzaa
celebrate
harvest
candle
candleholder

Materials

seven cardboard toilet tissue rolls covered with construction paper: three red, three green and one black
red, green and black construction paper candles the same height as the toilet tissue rolls (made by cutting the paper to size, rolling it around a pencil, securing the ends with tape and slipping the pencil out), one per child
yellow construction paper to make candle flames for each candle

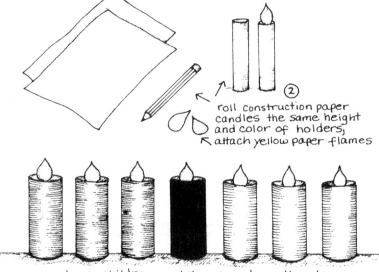

① ← cover seven rolls with construction paper; 3 red, 3 green, one black.

② roll construction paper candles the same height and color of holders, attach yellow paper flames

③ have children match colored candles to candle holders and place inside so flames are visable.

What to do

1. Discuss the meaning of Kwanzaa and how it is celebrated (see below).
2. Put the covered cardboard rolls on a hard, flat surface in this order—three red, one black, three green.
3. Hand out the candles and tell the children that we are going to light the Kwanzaa candles.
4. One at a time, have each child tell the class the color of his or her own candle and place it in the matching candleholder.
5. After all the children have put their candles in the holders, the yellow flames should be visible.

Want to do more?

Discuss with the children that learning about other cultures is interesting, helpful and fun.

Kwanzaa

Kwanzaa comes from the Kiswahili word "kwanza" which means "first." The essence of Kwanzaa is a true appreciation of Black people, building a sense of community and supporting common values.

DAY	PRINCIPLE	MEANING
December 26	Umoja	Unity
December 27	Kujuchagulia	Self-determination
December 28	Ujima	Collective work & responsibility
December 29	Ujamaa	Cooperative economics
December 30	Nia	Purpose
December 31	Kuumba	Creativity
January 1	Imani	Faith

There are seven symbols of Kwanzaa:

SYMBOL	SYMBOLISM
Mkeka (straw mat)	Foundations upon which all else rests
Kinara (candle holder)	Original stalk from which we all come—African ancestors
Mishumaa saba (7 candles)	Nguzo sabe—seven principles
Vibunzi (ears of corn)	Children—an ear for each child
Kikombe	Unity cup
Mazao (crops)	Fruits of our labor
Zawadi (gifts)	Rewards for our achievements

Lighting ceremony—Light one mishumaa each day symbolizing the principle of that day. Begin with the black candle, which represents the first principle, Umoja (unity). Each day after, alternately light the red and green candles. After each lighting, discuss with the children the principle of the day.

★ The Giant Encyclopedia of Theme Activities

Dramatic Play Activities

Post Office with Mail Boxes

3+

Children make a useful item, a mailbox, that they then use to receive mail from the other children.

Words to use

create
mailbox
letter
deliver

Materials

shoe boxes or
   cardboard tubes
markers or
   crayons
glue or tape

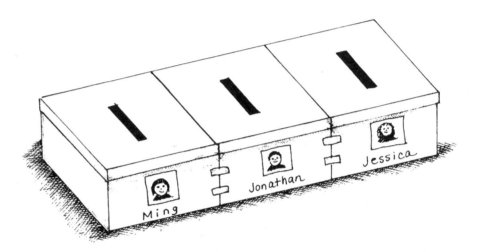

What to do

1. Encourage each child to make a mailbox in which to receive letters.
2. Make the mailboxes from shoe boxes or cardboard tubes.
3. Display each child's name and picture on the front of the box for easy letter delivery.
4. Glue or tape these mailboxes together so they will be durable for mail delivery by their classmates and teacher.

★ THE COMPLETE LEARNING CENTER BOOK

Postcards

3+

Encourages language and social skills.

Words to use

postcard
color
write
message
address

Materials

paper
scissors
markers and crayons
old greeting cards or postcards
tape

What to do

1. Make postcards for the Writing Center by having children cut up paper and draw picture stamps for the card. Children write messages on the opposite side of the picture.
2. Recycle old greeting cards or postcards by covering the address and message with blank paper. Children write new messages on the postcards.

★ THE COMPLETE LEARNING CENTER BOOK

Toy Puzzles   3+

Children feel a great sense of accomplishment when they make something other children can use.

Words to use

puzzle
picture
cut out

Materials

toy catalogs
scissors
Styrofoam trays
glue

What to do

1. Children cut out pictures of toys from catalogs and glue them on a Styrofoam tray.
2. After the pictures are dry they cut the tray into pieces.
3. They put the pictures back together or share the puzzle with a friend.

★ THE COMPLETE LEARNING CENTER BOOK

Toy Puppets

3+

Children use their imagination to create toy puppets.

Words to use

design
unique
decorate

Materials

Styrofoam cups, straws, pipe cleaners, old mittens, etc.
yarn, contact paper, buttons, trim, etc.
plastic basket
Alexander and the Wind-up Mouse by Leo Lionni, optional

What to do

1. The children create puppets using simple designs.
2. Each child keeps their materials in a plastic basket so he can create his own unique toy puppet.
3. Possible puppet materials include Styrofoam cups, straws, pipe cleaners, old mittens, construction paper, ice-cream sticks, felt shapes and glue.
4. Decorate with yarn, contact paper, buttons, trim.
5. If desired, make cardboard keys for a wind-up toy that relates to *Alexander and the Wind-up Mouse*.

★ THE COMPLETE LEARNING CENTER BOOK

Packing for Our Visit

3+

Children learn to pack clothes, toys and books.

Words to use

suitcase
backpack
visit
pack

Materials

suitcases, duffel bags, backpacks
clothing
telephone
toys
books

What to do

1. Place the suitcases, bags and backpacks in the housekeeping corner and observe the children's interactions.
2. Stimulate the play by calling the children on the telephone and pretending you are their grandmother. Invite them for a visit. Remind them to bring some toys and books, as well as clothes that fit the weather. Pretend you live far away.
3. When the children pretend that they arrive at your house, help them unpack, and discuss why they brought these particular clothes, toys and books.

Teaching tips

For younger children, pretend to be the mother or father helping the children get ready for a trip. For older children, stimulate play by posing the problem of what other travel preparations are needed for the family to leave home, such as finding a kennel for the family pet, getting someone to water the plants and stopping the paper delivery.

★ More Story S-t-r-e-t-c-h-e-r-s

Pilots and Flight Attendants   3+

Children will have fun dressing in the uniforms of pilots and flight attendants.

Words to use

flight attendant
pilot
uniforms

Materials

captain's hat from a commercial or military airline
blazers, scarves, aprons
plastic flight wings
serving carts
full length mirror

What to do

1. Ask for donations to the dress-up corner in your parent newsletter.
2. Encourage children who have not flown to play in the dress-up area with those who have.
3. Assist with dressing the flight attendants and have them model their outfits in front of the full length mirror.
4. Leave the flight attendants and pilots to manage the airplane on their own.

Teaching tips

Some dress-up clothes can serve double duty. The pilot's hat can also be a police officer's hat. The blazers can belong to flight attendants or be the dress-up clothes for the office. Parents are eager to help when they know why you need items. Grandparents often have some of the best items to donate. Take pictures of the children in the dress-up clothes and post them on the parent bulletin board or send pictures to the grandparents who donated the items.

★ Story S-t-r-e-t-c-h-e-r-s

Homemade Sleigh   3+

Develops imagination and coordination.

Words to use

sled
sleigh
create

Materials

large cardboard box (about
    12" x 18")
scissors
rope
bells, optional

What to do

1. Cut the top flaps off of the box. If the box is deep, cut it down so that it is no more than 4 to 6 inches high.
2. Make a hole in each of the long sides of the box about 2 inches from the corners. Insert a rope through each hole and knot it to make a pulling strap. Add bells if desired.
3. A few stuffed animals or dolls to pull in the sleigh will add to the fun.

★ Where Is Thumbkin?

Wrapping Presents

Encourages creativity, generosity and coordination.

Words to use

wrap
gift
bow
ribbon
decorate
present
holiday
celebrate
generosity
Thank you

Materials

a variety of boxes
recycled wrapping paper
bows
tape

What to do

1. Set up a gift wrapping section in the dramatic play center.
2. Let the children experiment with different wraps and bows.

★ WHERE IS THUMBKIN?

Language Activities

Menorah Flannel Pieces   3+

Teaches children to appreciate many cultures.

Words to use

menorah
Hanukkah
candle
flame

Materials

Menorah base, candles and flames cut from felt

What to do

1. Encourage the children to assemble the menorah on the flannel board.
2. During Hanukkah, add a flame each day until all eight candles are lit.

★ WHERE IS THUMBKIN?

The Mystery Food   3+

Teaches about the texture of food.

Words to use

fruit
vegetables
skin
feels like
texture
rough
smooth

Materials

apple (or orange, pepper, zucchini, banana, etc.)
coffee can
sock

What to do

1. Place an apple in the bottom of a coffee can.
2. Cover the can by stretching a sock over the top.
3. Let the children reach into the can, with the sock covering their hand.
4. Ask them to identify the fruit or vegetable inside the can by feeling it.
5. Ask questions like "Is it rough?" "Is it smooth?"
6. Ask each child not to tell what they think the object is until all the children have had a turn to feel what is inside the can.
7. Try oranges, peppers, zucchini and bananas.

★ 500 FIVE MINUTE GAMES

Writing About Our Travel Adventures   3+

Children learn to recall traveling with family and to see their spoken words becoming written words.

Words to use

remember   write
travel   trip

Materials

chart tablet or poster board
marker

What to do

1. Ask the children to recall some times when their families traveled together. Discuss their trips for a few minutes.
2. Tell the children that you want to remember what they have told you so you are going to write it down.
3. Have each child tell at least one sentence about a time when their family traveled together for a vacation or even a trip across town.
4. As you print their sentences on the chart tablet or poster board, repeat what the child has said so that the children can observe spoken language becoming written language.
5. After each child's sentence is printed, reread the sentence in a fluent way and run your fingers or a pointer under the words.
6. When the chart is finished, reread all of the traveling statements.

Teaching tips

In communities where families have little money for traveling, emphasize the many different forms of transportation the children see in their city or town.

★ MORE STORY S-T-R-E-T-C-H-E-R-S

language activities

Flannel Board Story Box

4+

Children develop language and social skills and an appreciation of books, stories and storytelling.

Words to use

story
felt
flannel board
characters

Materials

black felt
cigar box or any box with a flip top,
  one per child
paint
crayons
contact paper
glue
scissors

What to do

1. If appropriate, make the boxes with the children, or each child can make their own box. The children use the boxes with flannel board stories.
2. Have children decorate the outside of boxes with paint, crayons, colored contact paper or the medium of their choice.
3. Glue a piece of black felt to the inside of the flip top.
4. Provide children with their favorite flannel story characters and shapes to use on the flannel board story box. Pieces can be conveniently stored inside the box and won't get lost.
5. Sit back and enjoy the children's creative variations on their favorite stories.

Want to do more?

Teacher-made flannel board boxes can be put in the language area, along with story pieces for independent play by the children. Numbered fingerplays such as "Five Little Monkeys" can be made into flannel board pieces and used on the box to practice math skills.

Books to read

The Very Hungry Caterpillar by Eric Carle
The Very Busy Spider by Eric Carle
The Little Old Lady Who Swallowed a Fly by Ladybird Books
The Mitten by Jan Brett
Brown Bear, Brown Bear by Bill Martin, Jr.

★ THE GIANT ENCYCLOPEDIA OF THEME ACTIVITIES

Mystery Package

How can you describe something you can't see? This activity develops critical thinking.

Words to use

guess
shake
package
think
clue
wrapped up
hiding
sounds like

Materials

wrapping paper
boxes
tape
ribbon
several small inexpensive items—pieces of gum, plastic car, marbles

What to do

1. For several days, without the children seeing, wrap a small item and place it in the language center.
2. Allow the children to shake the boxes.
3. Provide clues, one at a time, as to what is inside the package.
4. Keep each item wrapped until someone guesses what is inside.
5. Let the "guesser" open the package and keep its contents.

★ Where Is Thumbkin?

Math Activities

Replicating Patterns with Blocks 3+

Children will learn to observe and replicate a friend's building structures.

Words to use

build
blocks
structure
same as
just like

Materials

We Are Best Friends by Aliki
small wooden blocks or plastic connecting blocks
toy cars and trucks

What to do

1. Show the illustrations from *We Are Best Friends* of the boys building block structures and playing with the toy cars and trucks.
2. Build a simple structure with blocks and ask a child to build another one just like it.
3. Pairs of children can build structures, with one child as builder and the second as replicator. Then they can switch roles.

Teaching tips

Younger children will place blocks end on end to create a train and other linear structures, while older children may use a variety of ways to replicate their friend's work, adding a block at a time or completing a structure.

★ MORE STORY S-T-R-E-T-C-H-E-R-S

Paper Chains

Children learn about patterning while developing their fine motor skills.

Words to use

chain
circle
loop
glue
attach
pattern

Materials

red and green construction paper
scissors
glue

What to do

1. Cut construction paper into 1 x 9 inch strips.
2. Loop a strip into a circle and glue it at the seam.
3. Place a second loop through the first and continue the chain.
4. The children can create their own color patterns.

★ WHERE IS THUMBKIN?

Tree Seriation

3+

Children explore the concept of sequencing.

Words to use

smallest
largest
in-between
size
tree
differences

Materials

construction paper trees cut in a variety of sizes

What to do

1. The children arrange the trees from smallest to largest.
2. Differences in size can be more subtle for older children.

★ WHERE IS THUMBKIN?

Five Little Candy Canes   3+

In this activity, children practice counting from one to five by doing a fingerplay.

Words to use

candy cane
first
second
third
fourth
fifth

Materials

flannel board
white and red felt for candy cane shapes

What to do

1. Make five candy canes by cutting white felt into candy cane shapes, approximately 1 x 4 inches. Cut five red strips, approximately 1/2 x 1 inch long, and glue on white candy canes.
2. Memorize the following fingerplay:

> *Five little candy canes*
> *Hanging from a Christmas tree.*
> *The first one said: "Children really do love me."*
> *The second one said: "Santa's coming here tonight."*
> *The third one said: "Christmas is such a delight."*
> *The fourth one said: "Look, it's Santa that I see."*
> *The fifth one whispered: "Santa's resting by our tree."*
> *So very, very softly, the candy canes did say,*
> *"Have a very Merry Christmas and a Happy Holiday."*

3. Introduce the activity to children and recite the poem.
4. Recite the poem again while putting the candy canes on the flannel board.
5. Have children do the fingerplay as you point to each candy cane on the board.
6. Have children count candy canes and number of stripes on each candy cane.
7. Repeat the fingerplay and take candy canes off the flannel board as each verse is said.

Want to do more?

Have each child make five candy canes out of red and white construction paper.

★ THE GIANT ENCYCLOPEDIA OF THEME ACTIVITIES

Ten Little Reindeer

3+

Teaches children counting skills.

Words to use

peek
surprise
reindeer

skip
rooftop

Materials

What to do

During the winter, especially around Christmas time, children love acting out this poem.

> *Peeking through the window, what do I see? (cup hands in front of eyes
>   to peek)*
> *One little, two little, three little reindeer. (raise one finger for each number)*
> *Skipping through the sky with a clickety click,*
> *Four little, five little, six little reindeer. (raise one finger for each number)*
> *Better go to bed,*
> *Better close my eyes, (close eyes)*
> *If I want a big surprise!*
> *Listen to the rooftop, what do I hear?*
> *Seven little, eight little, nine little, ten little reindeer.*
> > *Jackie Silberg*

★ 500 Five Minute Games

Counting Bags

4+

Children explore the concept of seriation.

Words

jingle bells
Velcro
comes after

lowest
highest
pocket

Materials

felt
15 jingle bells (available at craft or hobby stores)
stick-on numbers
glue gun
Velcro

What to do

1. Cut two 3-inch squares of felt.
2. Use a glue gun to glue the two pieces together on three sides, creating a pocket or bag.
3. Attach a 1-inch piece of Velcro just inside the top of each pocket/bag.
4. Place stick-on numbers from 1 to 5 on each bag.
5. The children place the appropriate number of bells into each bag.
6. The children can also place the bags into appropriate order by weight (lightest to heaviest), by sound (lowest to highest) or in numerical sequence.

★ WHERE IS THUMBKIN?

Christmas Tree Decorating   4+

Encourages counting skills.

Words to use

green   yellow
tree   numeral

Materials

green and red construction paper
yellow felt
scissors

What to do

1. Cut out five trees from green construction paper and yellow stars from felt.
2. Glue a star at the top of each tree and number them from one to five.
3. Cut out fifteen small red balls or circles. Have the children place as many red balls on the trees as specified by the numeral on the stars.
Note: This activity could also be used for other seasons—pumpkins for Halloween and bunnies for Spring, for example.

★ THE INSTANT CURRICULUM

Christmas Egg Carton Tree

Children learn about math, numbers, sharing and how to have a creative experience while developing fine motor skills.

Words to use

carton
egg cup
trunk
tree

Materials

Styrofoam egg cartons in different
  colors
poster board
glitter
scissors
glue

What to do

1. Cut egg cups from all egg cartons for a total of seventeen egg cups.
2. Glue one egg cup one inch from the top in the center of the poster board.
3. Immediately beneath the single cup, glue two more, one on either side. Continue the pattern with a row of three, four and five.
4. Ask the children what shape has been made.
5. Glue the two remaining egg cups vertically to form the trunk of the tree.
6. Put glitter on the tree for a festive look.

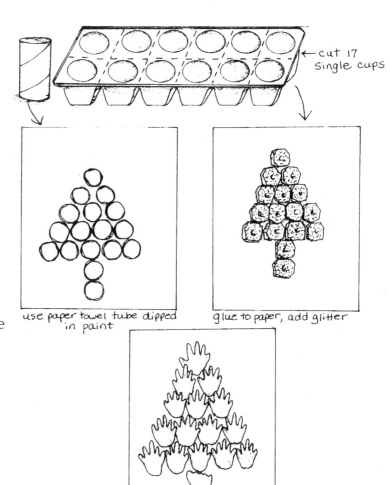

cut 17 single cups

use paper towel tube dipped in paint

glue to paper, add glitter

use children's handprints and a footprint for trunk

Want to do more?

Use a toilet paper or paper towel tube dipped in paint to print rows of increasing size in the pattern indicated above. Use hand prints similarly. Use a footprint for the tree trunk.

★ THE GIANT ENCYCLOPEDIA OF THEME ACTIVITIES

Eight

5+

Children explore the number eight, a number important to the holiday of Hanukkah.

Words to use

eight
Hanukkah
candles
count
objects
number

Materials

paper plates
odds and ends—bottle caps, paper clips, crayons, candles, pennies, marbles, etc.

What to do

1. Remind the children about the significance of the number eight to Hanukkah.
2. The children count eight items into each plate.

★ WHERE IS THUMBKIN?

Music and Movement Activities

Freckles and Stripes

3+

Children learn about the tempo of music.

Words to use

tempo
fast
slow
dots
stripe
line
long
short

Materials

crayons
paper

What to do

1. Provide each child with a variety of crayons and paper.
2. Play a record with a fast tempo and have children make dots on their paper in time with the music.
3. Play a record with a slow tempo and have them make stripes with the sides of their crayon.
4. Continue by playing both types of records, having children listen and decide whether it's freckle or stripe music before they use their crayons.

★ THE INSTANT CURRICULUM

Circles to Music

3+

Improves children's coordination.

Words to use

circles
round
rhythm
music
interpret
designs

Materials

paper
crayons

What to do

1. Provide each child with paper and crayons.
2. Play a record.
3. Ask the children to make circles to the rhythm of the music being played.
4. Intermittently stop the record and ask the children to change to another color of crayon.
5. The children will create a design of colorful circles, with a variety of interpretations.

★ THE INSTANT CURRICULUM

Crescendo

3+

Children learn that a crescendo starts soft and gets louder.

Words to use

crescendo
soft
loud

Materials

What to do

1. As children sing a song, use word clues (say "soft," "a little louder," etc.) to lead children through a song singing from very softly to softly to moderately loud to loud.
2. Using the same clues, lead them back down from loud to soft.
3. Teacher may reinforce word clues with facial expressions and ever widening or diminishing space between her hands.

★ THE INSTANT CURRICULUM

Imaginary Dancing

3+

Children learn to move in response to the music.

Words to use

glide
sway
dance

Materials

piano, or cassette or record player and recording of waltz music

What to do

1. Have the children remove shoes so they can glide more easily.
2. Begin by having the children simply sway in response to the music.
3. Then begin moving slowly around the room, stopping periodically to allow the children to listen and sway, then move again.

Teaching tips

If you have a child who has difficulty moving rhythmically, take both of the child's hands, and sway back and forth until he or she seems to feel the music.

★ STORY S-T-R-E-T-C-H-E-R-S

Reaching, Stretching, Growing, Knowing

3+

Children learn to chant with the motions.

Words to use

reach	stretch
grow	know
chant	move
tap	remember
short	tall
little	big

Materials

What to do

Use motions of reaching up with arms, pointing to self, indicating short and tall with hands and tapping temple to show remembering.

> *Reach-ing, stretch-ing, grow-ing, know-ing.*
> *I'm not little, I'm so big.*
> *I'm the growingest one of all.*
> *Reach-ing, stretch-ing, grow-ing, know-ing.*
> *I'm not short, I'm so tall.*
> *Reach-ing, stretch-ing, grow-ing, know-ing.*
> *I didn't forget, I remembered*
> *I'm the growingest one of all.*
> *(Repeat first stanza)*
>
> By Shirley Raines

Teaching tips

Make up your own tune to the chant and sing it for a song. Record your chant and let the children take the tape home to play.

★ Story S-t-r-e-t-c-h-e-r-s

Partner Kickball   5+

As children move through school, their self-confidence can be weakened as their achievements become more exclusively associated with winning. This game encourages cooperation not competition.

Words to use

cooperate
goal
partner
teamwork
together
kick
timer

Materials

medium-size box
large, soft ball
15" strip of cloth
timer
sponge

What to do

1. Ask the children to find a partner. Tell them you would like to see how well they cooperate to kick a ball into a goal. They will have to work together because one leg will be tied to their partner's.
2. Set the box on its side at one end of the room. Ask the partners to line up at the opposite end. Place the right leg of one partner and the left leg of the other close together and tie securely, but not too tightly, at the ankle with the strip of cloth and the sponge between their ankles as a cushion.
3. Set the ball in front of the two children and tell them the object of the game is to kick the ball with their tied legs into the box on the other side of the room before the timer goes off.
4. Set the timer for about three minutes and ask the children to begin.
5. When the timer goes off or they reach the goal, repeat with the second pair in the line.

Want to do more?

To change the level of difficulty, increase or decrease the size of the box and/or the ball. Try having two pairs of children kick two balls into the same box. When one pair is successful, they can go help the other. For a real challenge, tell the children to kick the ball backwards.

Home connection

Parents and children can play "Partner Kickball" at home.

★ THE PEACEFUL CLASSROOM

Science Activities

Weather Vanes

3+

Children construct a weather vane that will show the direction the wind is blowing.

Words to use

wind
blow
direction
weather vane
spin
turn
arrow
point

Materials

paper towel or toilet tissue rolls
scraps of poster board or any light weight cardboard that has layers
scissors
straight pins or long needles
thimble
tape

What to do

1. Cut a demonstration arrow from a piece of poster board or cardboard that is about two inches long and one inch wide.
2. Let each child cut an arrow shape. Do not be concerned if the arrow is not exact.
3. With a thimble, press a straight pin through the arrow and into the top of the paper towel or toilet tissue roll, leaving it loose enough to turn. (Supervise closely.)
4. Show the children how to blow on their weather vanes. Ask them which direction the arrow is pointing when it stops. It always points toward the source of the wind, the child.
5. To send the weather vanes home, take off the arrow and pin and tape them onto the side of the roll, covering the pin entirely with tape.

Teaching tips

Ask a parent or grandparent who is a gardener to bring in a garden pinwheel or weather vane. Some are often shaped like a bird with wings that rotate or like a flower with petals that rotate.

★ More Story S-t-r-e-t-c-h-e-r-s

Hot Bubble Fliers

Grab a bottle of warmed bubble solution, take your warm breath, and out you go to send hot air bubbles up into the cold sky. Cold air is heavier than warm air. Air rises as it gets warm and cold air moves in to take its place. This causes currents of air to move around inside as well as out of doors. The bubbles we blow on a cold winter day will float upward as the warm air inside rises.

Words to use

bubbles	warm
air	temperature
high	quickly
fast	lighter
cold	moves
replaces	float
rising	currents
breath	

Materials

bubble mixture (1/3 cup dish soap such as Dawn, 1 cup warm water and 1 teaspoon sugar)
container for mixture
bubble blowers

What to do

1. Let children mix bubble mixture indoors.
2. Go outside on a cold winter day and let them blow bubbles.
3. Observe the bubbles as they float upward.
4. Explain that the child's warm breath makes the bubbles very light and that cold air is heavier than warm air.
5. Why do the bubbles fly up so quickly? How high will they fly? Watch and see.

Want to do more?

Try the same experiment using cold water, approximately the same temperature as the outdoor air. What happens? Compare the two types of Bubble Fliers. Experiment with various bubble blowers. Does the type you use make a difference?

★ MORE MUDPIES TO MAGNETS

science activities

Magnetic Rice   3+

Children learn to locate objects that are attracted by the magnet.

Words to use

magnet
attracted to

Materials

large sheet cake baking pan
two or three pounds of rice
small metal objects—toy car, screw, nuts and bolts, scissors
other nonmagnetic objects—puzzle pieces, chalk, plastic blocks
large magnet

What to do

1. Place the objects in a random pattern in the bottom of the cake pan.
2. Pour enough rice over the top of the objects to just cover them.
3. When children come to the science corner during free play to investigate what has been added to the area, demonstrate how the magnet will pick up an object hidden under the rice. Find objects by moving the magnet just barely over the surface.
4. Have the children find the other objects that are magnetic.

Teaching tips

After the children have experience with magnets, select new objects and have the children predict which ones will be attracted to the magnet. Then have them test their predictions by burying the objects in the rice and using the magnet to search.
(Adapted from Suzanne Gray's classroom at George Mason University's Project for the Study of Young Children.)

★ Story S-t-r-e-t-c-h-e-r-s

Christmas Potpourri   3+

Children develop environmental awareness while practicing fine motor skills.

Words to use

needles
potpourri
cinnamon
nutmeg
bundle

Materials

pine tree needles
cinnamon sticks cut into 1/2″ pieces
nutmeg
small pine cones
netting
ribbon

What to do

1. The children place a mixture of pine needles, cinnamon sticks, nutmeg and pine cones on a piece of netting. Bundle together and tie.
2. Hang potpourri bundles around the classroom to create Christmas smells.
3. Explain to the children that this is a natural way to create a pleasant smell without harming the environment.

★ WHERE IS THUMBKIN?

Mirror Skating   4+

Children explore the properties of magnets.

Words to use

magnet
attract
top
surface
skate

Materials

small hand-held mirror
magnets, any size
magnetic wands

What to do

1. Hold the mirror horizontally in one hand.
2. Put a magnet on the top surface of the mirror.
3. Hold the wand in the other hand and run it along under the mirror to make the magnet on top "skate" around.

Want to do more?

Use different sizes and weights of magnets on the top and bottom. Put more than one magnet on top of the mirror and move them around.

★ THEMESTORMING

Balancing and Spinning   4+

Children explore and discover the concept of balancing.

Words to use

balance
top
spinning

Materials

a collection of items—tops, coins, spools, etc.
a straw

What to do

1. Show the children how to balance a straw across the tip of their finger. Explain that when a top is spinning, it is balanced on its tip.
2. Let the children try to balance a straw across a finger.
3. Next, give the children various items—tops, coins, spools—to spin.

★ WHERE IS THUMBKIN?

How Fast Does Your Crystal Grow?   4+

Crystals are found in igneous rocks. This activity demonstrates one way in which crystals can be grown. They form as water evaporates from the solution saturated materials that are provided below. With a little care, children can grow huge formations of crystals.

Words to use

crystals   igneous
rocks   sparkling
hard   soft
evaporate

Materials

four 1" square cubes cut from
    rubber sponge
ammonia
salt
water
liquid bluing
pie pan (glass or aluminum)
measuring cup
spoon

What to do

1. Place 1-inch square cubes of rubber sponge in the pie pan.
2. Pour the following materials in amounts designated into the pie pan.

> *1/4 cup water*
> *4 tablespoons table salt*
> *4 tablespoons bluing*
> *1 tablespoon ammonia*

Note: When mixing these materials, supervise closely.

3. Stir and spoon the mixture over the sponges until they are thoroughly soaked.
4. Place the pie pan on a table near a window.
5. Have the children make observations of the mixture every two hours. The crystallization begins immediately; however, it is most noticeable after an overnight soak. Then the crystals will grow continuously like plants with the look of coral. By adding small amounts of water on the third day, this phenomenon of crystallization can be observed for a week or longer.

Want to do more?

Crystals can be grown from such common substances as salt or alum. Mix water with these substances and compare the crystal growth to each other. Put in a cold, dry place, crystals grow bigger. The slower the evaporation, the bigger the crystals.

★ MORE MUDPIES TO MAGNETS

String Kabobs   4+

Children learn to care for animals.

Words to use

string
scraps
eat
birds

Materials

string
fat from meat
fruit peels
whole peanuts
round dry cereal

What to do

1. Have the children tie the string around or through food scraps to form a string kabob about twelve to eighteen inches long.
2. Hang the kabob from a tree branch.
3. Enjoy watching the birds eat their meal.

★ THEMESTORMING

Take a Bird to Lunch   5+

Our friends the birds need to eat just as we do. Tending a bird feeder helps children develop an interest in and a love for birds. It also provides an opportunity to identify different species of birds, their style of feeding and what they like to eat.

Words to use

feeding station
bird feeder
identify
appropriate bird names

Materials

an empty plastic milk or bleach bottle
    or
a small wooden board with molding of
    some type nailed around the edges
    to prevent the food from blowing
    away
a water dish
grains
dry cereals
all types of seeds
cracker crumbs, etc.

What to do

1. Build a bird feeder using a plastic milk bottle or a wooden board.
2. Attach the feeder to the outside ledge of the window or on a visible tree branch. Place different kinds of food on the feeder. Put a water dish out as well.
3. Caution the children not to make sudden movements as they watch the birds feed.
4. The adult should identify the birds for the children using pictures and manuals.
5. Observe the kinds of foods different birds eat.
6. Observe the total number of birds that come to the feeder.
7. Observe how long different birds stay at the feeder.
8. Observe the ground feeding birds.

★ HUG A TREE

Snack and Cooking Activities

Orange You Glad They're Not All Alike?   3+

While it is true that most children love to eat, what they love to eat may be another matter altogether. Tasting small amounts in the interest of science may entice some of those less eager eaters to try something new. It also gives them some experience with classification and sensory awareness.

Words to use

color   texture
taste   senses
same   different
fruit   root
vegetable   raw
cooked

Materials

orange fruits and vegetables such as oranges, carrots, mango, pumpkin, winter squash, melon,
    tangerines, orange tomatoes, peaches, apricots, tomato macaroni or noodles
knife
plates
napkins

What to do

1. Cut the food into small pieces so that each child has a sample of each food. Leave one of each item whole so the children can refer to it. The number of foods you use depends upon the experience of the children as well as availability. With very inexperienced children, you may want to compare only two items. Other children may enjoy working with as many as you can find.
2. Talk about what is the same about all the things on the plate—they're all orange, all little, all food.... Can you name any of them? Which ones look almost alike? Put the ones that look alike together. Do they smell alike? Do they taste alike? How are they different? Write down some of your findings.
3. Match the samples to the whole foods. Talk about which ones you've tasted and how they have been prepared. Eat the samples. Did they all taste good?

Want to do more?

Repeat with other food combinations. Play mystery food—guess what is on the plate by looking, smelling or tasting. You may want to use blindfolds. Sort by similar color, texture, taste, shape or whatever else comes to mind. Compare foods cooked and raw. Show the children pictures of the foods growing or better yet, see them in a garden. Do plants that are similar grow the same way? How many ways can the same food be prepared?

★ Mudpies to Magnets

Good and Juicy

3+

By using the blender to make flavorful slushes, you are actually creating a suspension. Once the ice has melted, the suspended solids of the vegetable or fruit will settle to the bottom. That's why we give juice a shake before we drink it.

Words to use

cut up	add
mix	blend
taste	combinations
suspension	fruit
vegetable	

Materials

blender
knife
crushed ice
assorted fruits such as bananas, dates, oranges, strawberries, watermelon, raspberries, pineapple, apples, tangerines, pears, apricots
assorted vegetables such as tomatoes, green peppers, peeled cucumbers, peeled zucchini
drinking glasses

What to do

1. Bring a variety of fruits and vegetables to the class. Discuss and share them, emphasizing that they belong to the fruit and vegetable food group. Separate them and identify the items as fruit or vegetable. Pass the foods around and talk about color, shape, firmness, texture and smell.
2. Explain that juices come from these foods. What juices are the children acquainted with? You may want to bring in cans as samples for each. How do fruits and vegetables become juices?
3. Have the children wash their hands.
4. Place vegetables and fruits in a pan or tub and have the children wash them.
5. Cut up the ripe fruit and vegetables.
6. Place 1/2 cup fruit in a blender with 1/4 cup crushed or cracked ice. Blend until smooth. Before blending, ask the children to predict what they think food items will look like, taste like and smell like after blending.
7. Pour finished product into juice glasses. Observe colors. Are they different than the original whole food item? Why?
8. Drink the juice and discuss its taste. Experiment with combining fruits, allowing children to make their own choices. Experiment with combining vegetables. Discuss likes and dislikes.

Want to do more?

Why are juices frozen when we buy them at the store? Have a juice party for parents to show one way to provide nutritious snacks for the entire family. Using a juicer will allow you to experiment with solid vegetables such as beets, celery, carrots and green peppers. Make a vegetable cocktail by juicing a variety of vegetables together. Freeze all the fruits and blend them without ice. What happens? Make fruit salad and vegetable salad. Talk about how fruits and vegetables grow. Show pictures or look at the actual plants. You can freeze some of the blended fruit in ice cube trays or small paper cups to make ice pops.

★ MUDPIES TO MAGNETS

Latkes

Children learn to appreciate a seasonal holiday food.

Words to use

Hanukkah
latkes
pancakes

Materials

grater
mixing bowl and spoon
1 teaspoon salt
1 egg
cooking oil
electric frying pan
applesauce
bowls

measuring spoons
1 grated onion
6 medium potatoes (washed, pared and grated)
3 tablespoons flour
1/2 teaspoon baking powder
paper towels
spoons

What to do

1. Mix the onion, salt and egg with the potatoes.
2. Add flour and baking powder.
3. Drop by spoonfuls into the hot oiled frying pan. (Supervise closely.)
4. Brown on both sides.
5. Drain on paper towels.
6. Serve with applesauce. Enjoy!

★ WHERE IS THUMBKIN?

Sugar Cookies

3+

Children learn creative expression.

Words to use

dough
cookie cutter
decorate

Materials

sugar cookie dough
sprinkles
Christmas cookie cutters
cookie sheets
oven
decorations, optional

What to do

1. Help the children cut shapes from the cookie dough and decorate as desired.
2. Bake and eat.

★ WHERE IS THUMBKIN?

Decorating with Food Coloring   3+

Children learn to mix food coloring to make a variety of new colors.

Words to use

color
mix
spread
icing
frosting
cracker
taste
sweet

Materials

two or three packages of food coloring, depending on how many children will be at the snack table
    at once
small plates or bowls
white cake icing
graham crackers
small plastic knives

What to do

1. Discuss with the children that the tops of food coloring bottles indicate the color inside, not the
   color of the liquid, which looks almost black.
2. Using only the selected primary colors for the day, such as blue and red, demonstrate how to mix
   the colors a drop at a time into the white cake icing and then stir.
3. Let each child place a small amount of icing into his bowl, then mix the colors.
4. Have the children spread a small amount of icing onto their graham crackers for snack time.

Teaching tip

Encourage the children's experimentation rather than exact color mixing.

★ MORE STORY S-T-R-E-T-C-H-E-R-S

Bread Sculptures

Bread dough is a great sculpture material, and when it's cooked, it's great to eat!

Words to use

dough   sculpt
knead   rise

Materials

1 tablespoon or 1 package dry yeast
1 cup water
1 teaspoon sugar
mixing bowls and wooden spoon
2 cups flour plus extra
1 tablespoon oil
1 teaspoon salt
400°F oven
cooling rack
kitchen tools for modeling (knife, fork,
     toothpick)
clean towel

What to do

1. Wash hands before beginning. Mix the
   water, sugar and yeast in a bowl until the
   yeast softens (about two to three minutes).
2. Add one cup of flour and stir vigorously
   with a wooden spoon. Beat the mixture until smooth and add one tablespoon of oil and one teaspoon of salt. Next add the second cup of flour to the dough.
3. Pour the thick batter onto a floured board and add more flour slowly while kneading the dough.
   Keep a coating of flour on the dough to prevent sticking.
4. Knead for about five minutes. The dough should be smooth, elastic and satiny and should bounce
   back if a finger is poked into it. Place the dough in an oiled bowl and cover with a clean towel. Set
   the bowl in a warm place for dough to rise for about forty-five minutes.
5. Punch the dough down and work it into a smooth ball. Divide the dough into portions for various
   parts of the bread sculpture or for different children to use.
6. Create sculptures with the dough. Create any shapes or designs.
7. Bake the sculptures for fifteen or twenty minutes in the lower part of a 400°F oven. Large forms
   may take longer. Bake until golden and baked through. Cool the sculptures on a rack. Eat and enjoy.

Teaching tips

Bread dough sculptures work well for holidays. Young artists like to keep a small bowl of flour handy
to keep their hands powdery while working. Sometimes they like the soft flour better than the
sculptures.

★ Preschool Art

Transition Activities

Jump Three Times   3+

Encourages children to practice jumping skills and counting skills.

Words to use

jump
three times
count

Materials

What to do

1. This is a good game for bridging from one activity to the next.
2. Ask the children to stand in a circle.
3. Tell them that when their turn comes, they should jump three times and count out loud as they jump.
4. Demonstrate how to do this.
5. When they are finished jumping, they may go to ... (the next activity).

★ 500 FIVE MINUTE GAMES

Here Come the Robots   3+

This activity encourages children to practice creative thinking.

Words to use

robot   pretend
move   conversation
talk like   game
sounds

Materials

What to do

1. Play a robot game.
2. The children pretend to be robots and move their bodies accordingly.
3. Pretend their arms and legs make sounds.
4. Talk like robots and invent conversations.
5. This game offers a good transition from one activity to another.

★ 500 FIVE MINUTE GAMES

Lollipops   3+

Use lollipops while waiting for children to clean up, wash hands or between activities. Singing makes everyone feel good, while enhancing language, auditory memory and motor skills. These lollipops also encourage children to use pictures as clues and to associate print with the song titles.

Words to use

songs
sing
favorite
choose

Materials

poster board scraps (different colors)
markers
scissors
popsicle sticks
cup or can
glue or tape

What to do

1. Cut 3-inch circles from the poster board.
2. Write the titles of the class's favorite songs, chants or finger-plays on the circles. Draw a picture related to the song.
3. Glue or tape the circles to popsicle sticks to make lollipops and store in a can or cup.
4. When there are a few extra minutes, choose a child to pull out a lollipop.
5. Sing or say that song, fingerplay or chant.

Want to do more?

Play "Name That Tune." Let one child hum a tune for the other children to guess. Older children could make and illustrate their own lollipops.

★ TRANSITION TIME

transition activities

Make a Lap

3+

This little poem helps children sit down or stand up. When children repeat the words and do the motions, they settle down.

Words to use

head	nose
ear	toes
clap	lap

Materials

What to do

1. Ask the children to repeat each line.
2. Model the motions for the children.

> *I tap my head.*
> *I push my nose.*
> *I pull my ear.*
> *I touch my toes.*
> *I clap, clap, clap.*
> *Then I sit down*
> *And make my lap.*

Want to do more?

If children are sitting, say this verse to get them to stand up.

> *I tap my head.*
> *I push my nose.*
> *I pull my ear.*
> *I touch my toes.*
> *I clap, clap, clap.*
> *Then I stand up.*
> *Uh, oh, where's my lap?*

Sing this song to the tune of "If You're Happy and You Know It," to encourage children to sit down.

> *Put your bottom on the rug, on the rug.*
> *Put your bottom on the rug, on the rug.*
> *Put your bottom on the rug, then give yourself a hug,*
> *Put your bottom on the rug, on the rug.*

★ TRANSITION TIME

Coat Hanger Critter

Coat hanger puppets are a fun way to introduce new themes or concepts or to give children direction. Children enjoy listening to puppets and making up stories with puppets.

Words to use

puppet
critter
name

Materials

coat hanger
old nylon stockings
cloth tape
yarn, felt scraps, buttons, wiggly eyes, etc.
scissors
glue

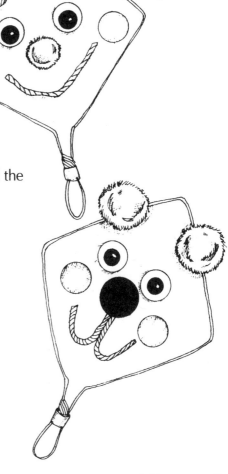

What to do

1. Stretch the hanger into a diamond shape as shown, then pull the stocking over it and tie at the bottom.
2. Bend the hook into an oval and tape it in place so it won't poke the children.
3. Decorate the puppet to look like one of the characters shown or create your own critters.
4. Hold up the puppet and ask the children to guess its name.
5. When a child says a name that suits the puppet, say, "Yes, you're right. How did you know?"
6. Next, let the puppet tell the children a story, share a new theme, give directions for a new game or activity, etc.

Want to do more?

Children will enjoy making their own coat hanger puppets to use in dramatizing stories or singing songs.

★ TRANSITION TIME

Art Parade   3+

Have an art parade when children complete an art project. Then, only a few minutes are needed to finish putting things away. Children love to "show off" their artwork and will have fun marching around the room.

Words to use

music
march
parade
artwork

Materials

record or tape with a bouncy beat

What to do

1. Tell the children they are going to have an art parade so everyone can see their pictures.
2. Let them get their paintings, collages, puppets or whatever they have made.
3. Help them pick up the art area while they get their artwork.
4. Choose a leader and have the others get in line.
5. Play the music as the children march around the room holding up their pictures.

Want to do more?

Visit other classrooms and show them your parade of art, or visit the school office or cafeteria. Let children take turns telling the other children the title of their artwork and describing how they made it.

★ TRANSITION TIME

Follow the Flashlight   3+

Use a flashlight to change the pace in the room and gather children in a group. As children follow along in this game, they are practicing visual tracking skills.

Words to use

flashlight
shine
imagine
quiet

Materials

flashlight

What to do

1. Turn off the lights.
2. Tell the children to get behind you and follow the trail the flashlight shines on the floor.
3. When the children are ready, walk around the room making an imaginary trail on the floor with the flashlight.
4. After walking around the room in a creative pattern, sit down quietly on the floor, turn off the flashlight and speak quietly to the children about what they will do next.

Want to do more?

To make different colors of light, cover the flashlight with colored cellophane held in place with a rubber band. Let the children hold the flashlight and shine a path for their friends to follow. Make designs on the ceiling with the flashlight. Let children make shadow animals on the wall with a flashlight or film projector.

★ TRANSITION TIME

Can You Name _____?

3+

Teaches children color recognition.

Words to use

color
favorite
song

Materials

What to do

1. Sing the following song to the tune of "London Bridge Is Falling Down."
2. Leave out the final word for a child to fill in.
3. If color is the subject, the song goes like this.

> *Can you name your favorite color,*
> *Favorite color, favorite color?*
> *Can you name your favorite color?*
> *(Tell us, Brian)*
>
> _____.

4. Brian names his favorite color.
5. Play this game using various subjects like trees, animals, flowers, food, etc.

★ 500 FIVE MINUTE GAMES

Mystery Music

3+

Teaches children listening skills.

Words to use

music
guess
song

Materials

What to do

1. Hum the melody of a familiar song or sing "la, la, la" instead of the words.
2. Ask the children to identify the song.
3. Repeat the song, stopping on a certain word.
4. See if they can identify that word.
5. Ask them what the next word of the song would be.

★ 500 Five Minute Games

Twinkle, Twinkle   3+

Teaches children about musical phrasing.

Words to use

beat
syllable

Materials

What to do

1. Sing "Twinkle, Twinkle, Little Star" and clap your hands to the syllables.
2. Clap for seven beats, and on the eighth beat, keep silent.
3. Tell the children to freeze on the eighth beat.

> *Twin-kle twin-kle lit-tle star*
> *clap-clap-clap-clap-clap-clap-clap (freeze)*
> *How-I won-der what-you are*
> *clap-clap-clap-clap-clap-clap-clap (freeze)*

4. Continue the same way with each line.
5. Instead of clapping, jump or stamp your feet.

★ 500 Five Minute Games

Jingle Bell Blanket

3+

Teaches children cooperation.

Words to use

jingle
up
down
bounce
together

Materials

blanket or sheet
small jingle bells

What to do

1. Ask the children to stand around the perimeter of a blanket and hold the blanket waist-high.
2. Place the jingle bells in the center of the blanket.
3. As the children sing "Jingle Bells," ask them to wave the blanket up and down to make the bells bounce and jingle on the blanket.
4. For a challenge, ask the children to try to keep the bells on the blanket without falling off throughout the singing of the song.

Want to do more?

Art: Small jingle bells can be purchased from craft stores and strung on strings to make jingle bell bracelets and necklaces. Older children can make jingle jars by placing pennies in baby food jars and screwing the lids on tightly.

Science: Place different size and types of bells in the discovery center for children to listen to and determine which make the loudest or softest sound and which has the highest or lowest pitch.

★ THE GIANT ENCYCLOPEDIA OF CIRCLE TIME AND GROUP ACTIVITIES

The Quiet Touch

4+

Children will enjoy this game whenever there are a few extra minutes. The game also develops visual memory and sequence skills.

Words to use

touch
sequence
order

Materials

What to do

1. The first child gets up, touches an object in the room, then sits down.
2. The second child gets up, touches what the first child touched, touches a second object, then sits down.
3. The game continues with each child touching the objects the previous children touched in sequential order, plus a new object at the end.
4. When a child misses, just begin a new game.

Want to do more?

Children enjoy the challenge of counting and seeing how may objects they can remember. A similar game can be played with children making various noises. When playing Noisy Touch, children might turn on the sink, shut the door, write on the board, move a chair, etc. Each child adds a new sound until the sequence is missed, then begin the game again.

★ TRANSITION TIME

Rubber Band   5+

Research shows that, over time, children may begin to prefer easy tasks to challenging ones. Fear of failure can erode the adventuresome spirit prevalent in young children.

Words to use

cooperate
teamwork
group

Materials

a rope equivalent in length to a line of all your children standing side by side

What to do

1. Tie the ends of the rope together.
2. Place the rope on the floor in a circle. Ask all the children to grab the rope and pick it up together. Ask them to face the center of the circle and take one step after another, backwards, until the rope is stretched as far as it will go.

3. Tell the children you would like to see how well they can cooperate. You would like them to move in the same direction, keeping the rope stretched as much as possible. Ask the group to move toward a nearby object.
4. Remind them that everyone has to work together to keep the rope stretched.
5. If the group moves successfully, ask them to cover more distance. Ask them to walk faster and then slower.

Want to do more?

For an added challenge, call the game "Rubber Band Leader." Ask one child to go to the center. The rest of the group has to keep the circle stretched around her as she walks. Can they keep the leader in the center? When you call out "Switch!" everyone drops the rope, runs to the center, then returns to a new spot in the circle. To add to the challenge, ask everyone to go inside the circle, raise the rope behind them and take steps backward until the rope is totally stretched. Ask them to let go of the rope with their hands. See if they can maintain the tension in the rope so that it will remain off the ground as they move as a group from one point to another.

Home connection

Parents and children can try "Rubber Band" at home, involving friends and relatives if needed to make a large enough group.

★ THE PEACEFUL CLASSROOM

Taste Helpers   5+

Although this activity is described to children as a guessing game, the primary emphasis is the gentle and helpful behavior children offer while feeding their partners. It also provides a safe situation for children to wear a blindfold. Check for food allergies before engaging in any food activity.

Words to use

helping
gentle
partners
trust

Materials

bowls of applesauce, pudding and fruit cocktail
bag of wooden or plastic spoons (about four per child)
paper cup with water for each child
blindfold

What to do

1. Tell the children you have a guessing game for them to play with a partner in the snack area. One partner wears a blindfold and the other selects one of three foods to feed the blindfolded partner.
2. Set out the bowls, spoons and cups of water. Invite children to find a partner.
3. Partners should sit close together, facing each other. Once sitting, the child who will taste the food should be gently blindfolded. Partners take a spoon and decide what to give the blindfolded child. Emphasize the gentle behavior needed for feeding.
4. After carefully tasting what their partner selected, the children guess what it is.
5. After tasting the three types of food, the partners switch roles.
6. Ask the children to take their time. They should taste the food carefully before guessing and drink water between samples. They should use a clean spoon each time.

Want to do more?

Make the activity more challenging by increasing the number of foods. Add variety by changing the types of foods. For example, offer five or six different types of raw vegetables or fruits.

Book to read

Vegetable Soup by Jeanne Modesitt

Home connection

Parents can repeat the activity at home. For example, one parent can select food for a child to feed the other blindfolded parent.

★ THE PEACEFUL CLASSROOM

Books

The Chanukka Guest by Eric Kimmel
Hanukah Money by Sholem Aleichem
Hanukkah by Norma Simon
Hanukkah by Roni Schotter
Hanukkah Story by Marilyn Hirsh
How the Grinch Stole Christmas by Dr. Seuss
Las Navidades: Popular Christmas Songs from Latin America by Lulu Delacre
Latkes and Applesauce by Fran Manushkin
Let's Play Dreidel by Roz Grossman and Gladys Gerwirtz
The Little Fir Tree by Margaret Wise Brown
Merry Christmas, Strega Nona by Tomie dePaola
My First Chanukah by Tomie dePaola
The Night Before Christmas by Clement C. Moore
The Polar Express by Van Allsburg
The Snowy Day by Ezra Jack Keats
The Twelve Days of Christmas by Jan Brett

Records, Tapes and CDs

Beall, Pamela Conn and Susan Hagen Nipp. "Christmas Is Coming" from *Wee Sing Children's Songs and Fingerplays*. Price Stern Sloan.
Gallina, Jill. *Holiday Songs for All Occasions*. Kimbo, 1978.
Palmer, Hap. *Holiday Songs and Rhythms*. Educational Activities, 1971.
Raffi. *Raffi's Christmas Album*. Shoreline, 1983.

JANUARY

Fingerplays, Poems and Songs

The North Wind Doth Blow

The north wind doth blow
And we shall have some snow.
And what will the robin do then, poor thing?
He will sit in the barn and keep himself warm,
With his little head tucked under his wing, poor
    thing!

★ ONE POTATO, TWO POTATO, THREE POTATO, FOUR

Snow, Snow, Fly Away

Snow, snow, fly away
Over the hills and far away.

★ ONE POTATO, TWO POTATO, THREE POTATO, FOUR

Frosty Weather, Snowy Weather

Frosty weather, snowy weather
When the wind blows,
We all go together.

★ ONE POTATO, TWO POTATO, THREE POTATO, FOUR

Polly, Put the Kettle On

Polly, put the kettle on,
Polly, put the kettle on,
Polly, put the kettle on;
We'll all have tea.

Sukey, take it off again,
Sukey, take it off again,
Sukey, take it off again;
They've all gone away.

★ ONE POTATO, TWO POTATO, THREE POTATO, FOUR

Sally Go Round the Sun

Sally, go round the sun.
Sally, go round the moon.
Sally, go round the chimney pots
On a Sunday afternoon.

★ ONE POTATO, TWO POTATO, THREE POTATO, FOUR

This Is a Snowman As Round As a Ball

This is a snowman as round as a ball.
He has two large eyes, but he's not very tall.
If the sun shines down on him today,
My jolly snowman will melt away.

★ ONE POTATO, TWO POTATO, THREE POTATO, FOUR

Snowmen

Five little snowmen
With buttons from the store.
This one melted,
And then there were four.
Four little snowmen beneath a pine tree.
This one melted,
And then there were three.
Three little snowmen
Glad that they know you.
This one melted
And then there were two.
Two little snowmen
Playing and having fun.
This one melted and then there was one.
One little snowman left all alone.
He melted all away,
And then there was none.

★ TRANSITION TIME

The Three Little Kittens

Three little kittens, they lost their mittens,
And they began to cry,
"Oh, Mother dear, see here, see here,
Our mittens we have lost!"
"What? Lost your mittens? You naughty kittens!
Then you shall have no pie."
"Meow! Meow! Meow! Meow!"

Three little kittens, they found their mittens,
And they began to cry,
"Oh, Mother dear, see here, see here,
Our mittens we have found!"
"What? Found your mittens? You darling kittens!
Then you shall have some pie."
"Meow! Meow! Meow! Meow!"

Three little kittens put on their mittens,
And soon ate up the pie.
"Oh, Mother dear, we greatly fear,
Our mittens we have soiled."
"What? Soiled your mittens? You naughty kittens!"
And they began to sigh,
"Meow! Meow! Meow! Meow!"

Three little kittens, they washed their mittens,
And hung them up to dry.
"Oh, Mother dear, see here, see here,
Our mittens we have washed!"
"What? Washed your mittens? You darling kit-
tens!
But I smell a mouse close by!
"Hush! Hush! Hush! Hush!"

★ WHERE IS THUMBKIN?

Peanut Butter

Chorus:
Peanut, peanut butter-Jelly,
Peanut, peanut butter-Jelly!

First you take the peanuts and you dig 'em, dig
'em
Dig 'em, dig 'em, dig 'em
Then you smash 'em, smash 'em,
Smash 'em, smash 'em, smash 'em,
Then you spread 'em, spread 'em,
Spread 'em, spread 'em, spread 'em.

(Chorus)

Then you take the berries and you pick 'em,
   pick 'em
Pick 'em, pick 'em, pick 'em,
Then you smash 'em, smash 'em,
Smash 'em, smash 'em, smash 'em,
Then you spread 'em, spread 'em
Spread 'em, spread 'em, spread 'em

(Chorus)

Then you take the sandwich and you bite it, bite
   it
Bite it, bite it, bite it,
Then you chew it, chew it,
Chew it, chew it, chew it
Then you swallow it, swallow it, swallow it,
Swallow it, swallow it, swallow it.

(Hum chorus)

Peanut, peanut butter-Jelly,
Peanut, peanut butter-Jelly!

★ WHERE IS THUMBKIN?

The Fox

The fox went out in the chilly night,
He prayed for the moon to give him light;
He'd many a mile to go that night
Before he reached the town-o, town-o, town-o,
He'd many a mile to go that night
Before he reached the town-o.

He ran till he came to a great big bin,
The ducks and the geese were kept therein;
A couple of you will grease my chin
Before I leave this town-o...

So he grabbed a gray goose by the neck
And threw a duck across his back;
He didn't mind their "quack, quack, quack"
And their legs dangling down-o...

Then old Mother Flipper-flopper jumped out of
   bed
And out of the window she stuck her head;
Said, "John, John, the gray goose is gone,
And the fox is in the town-o...

So John he ran to the top of the hill
And he blew his horn both loud and shrill;
The fox he said, "I'd better flee with my kill
Or they'll soon be on my trail-o...

He ran till he came to his cozy den
And there were his little ones, eight, nine, and
   ten;
They said, "Daddy, you better go back again
'Cause it must be a mighty fine town-o"...

So the fox and wife, without any strife,
They cut up the goose with a fork and a knife;
They never had such a supper in their lives
And the little ones chewed on the bones-o...

★ WHERE IS THUMBKIN?

The Mulberry Bush

Here we go round the mulberry bush,
The mulberry bush, the mulberry bush,
Here we go round the mulberry bush,
So early in the morning.

This is the way we wash our clothes...
So early Monday morning.

This is the way we iron our clothes...
So early Tuesday morning.

This is the way we mend our clothes...
So early Wednesday morning.

This is the way we scrub the floor...
So early Thursday morning.

This is the way we sweep the house...
So early Friday morning.

This is the way we bake our bread...
So early Saturday morning.

This is the way we go to church...
So early Sunday morning.

★ WHERE IS THUMBKIN?

Where Is Thumbkin?

Where is thumbkin?
Where is thumbkin?
Here I am, Here I am;
How are you today, sir?
Very well, I thank you,
Run away, Run away.

Where is pointer?
Where is pointer?
Here I am, Here I am;
How are you today, sir?
Very well, I thank you,
Run away, Run away.

Where is middle finger?

Where is ring finger?

Where is pinky?

★ WHERE IS THUMBKIN?

January Learning Centers

Library Center

While playing in the Library Center children will learn:

1. To develop their interest in a variety of books, magazines and other printed materials.
2. That stories can be in many forms including books, magazines, tapes, flannel board stories and puppet shows.
3. To enjoy reading books and retelling stories.

Suggested props for the Library Center

a collection of children's books appropriate for the interest and developmental level of the children in the classroom—include a minimum of five books for each child that will be in the center at one time (five children in the center x five books = 25 books)

children's magazines (such as Ranger Rick, Ladybug, Big Backyard and Sesame Street)

cassette tape player (one that is easy for young children to use)

earphones (provides private listening opportunities)

books with tapes (kept together in resealable plastic bags)

flannel board with story pieces in plastic bags (used by children in retelling stories)

pillows that are soft and movable (such as lawn chair cushions)

posters of book characters or pictures of children reading (displayed in the area)

a stamp, ink pad and cards (to check books out)

a small table and chair (used when stamping books and signing names)

newspapers and "Mini Page" (children's newspaper section)

a large cardboard box (can be opened on one side to create a private reading space; a flashlight inside the box adds to the enticement of the area)

a lamp or clamp-on light (provides a well-lighted area for better reading)

an unusual item to draw interest to the area (a dome tent, a bath tub, a couch with legs cut off, a suspended parachute, a raised platform or an air mattress)

soft cuddly animals or teddy bears for snuggling when reading

Curriculum Connections

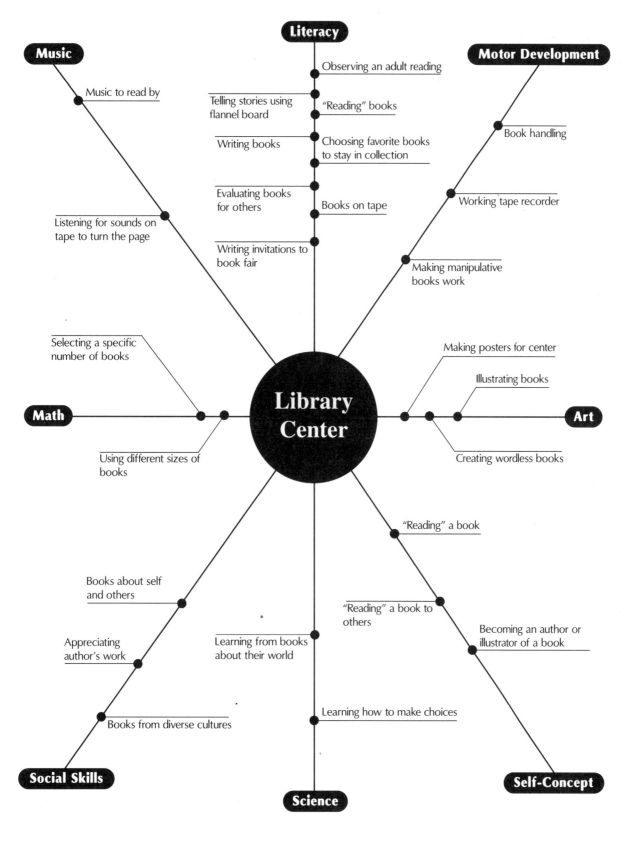

Literacy
- Observing an adult reading
- Telling stories using flannel board
- "Reading" books
- Writing books
- Choosing favorite books to stay in collection
- Evaluating books for others
- Books on tape
- Writing invitations to book fair

Music
- Music to read by
- Listening for sounds on tape to turn the page

Motor Development
- Book handling
- Working tape recorder
- Making manipulative books work

Math
- Selecting a specific number of books
- Using different sizes of books

Art
- Making posters for center
- Illustrating books
- Creating wordless books

Social Skills
- Books about self and others
- Appreciating author's work
- Books from diverse cultures

Science
- "Reading" a book
- "Reading" a book to others
- Learning from books about their world
- Learning how to make choices

Self-Concept
- Becoming an author or illustrator of a book

Library Center

★ THE COMPLETE LEARNING CENTER BOOK

Doctor's Office/Hospital Center

While playing in the Doctor's Office/Hospital Center children will learn:

1. About the services provided by health care professionals.
2. To use new vocabulary related to the doctor's office and hospitals.
3. To play different roles and appreciate the assistance these community helpers provide.
4. To alleviate some of their concerns and fears through socio-dramatic play.

Suggested props for the Doctor's Office/Hospital Center

computer/typewriter for office
clip boards
telephone
stethoscope
old x-rays
masks
gloves
wagon for moving hospital
   patients
prescription pads
lab jackets
first aid supplies such as
   bandages
   tape
   gauze
   scissors (blunt, if possible)
   cotton balls
   empty alcohol bottle
   empty antiseptic tubes
   soap

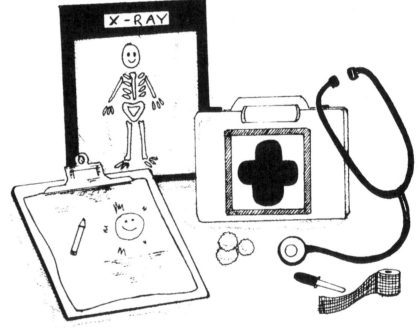

Curriculum Connections

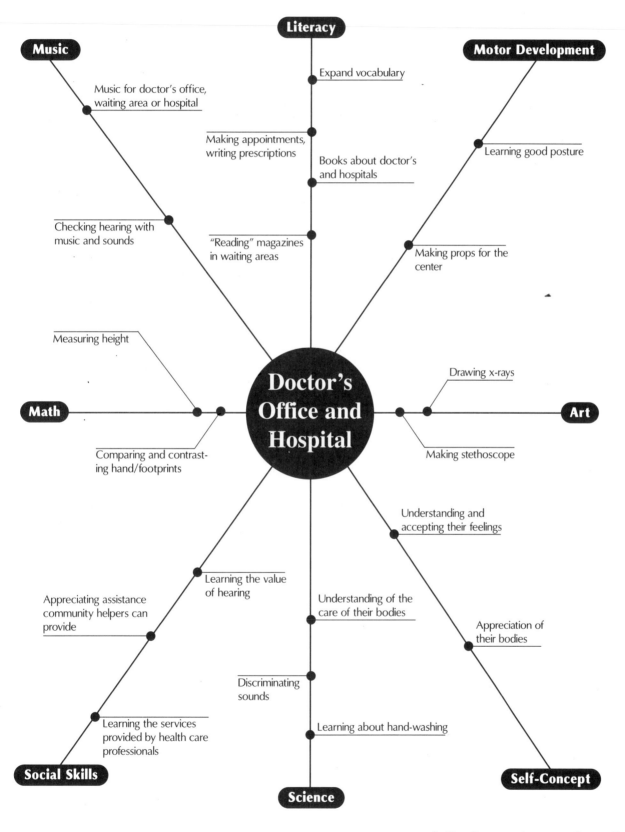

Literacy
- Expand vocabulary
- Making appointments, writing prescriptions
- Books about doctor's and hospitals
- "Reading" magazines in waiting areas

Music
- Music for doctor's office, waiting area or hospital
- Checking hearing with music and sounds

Motor Development
- Learning good posture
- Making props for the center

Math
- Measuring height
- Comparing and contrasting hand/footprints

Art
- Drawing x-rays
- Making stethoscope

Doctor's Office and Hospital

Social Skills
- Appreciating assistance community helpers can provide
- Learning the value of hearing
- Learning the services provided by health care professionals

Science
- Understanding of the care of their bodies
- Discriminating sounds
- Learning about hand-washing

Self-Concept
- Understanding and accepting their feelings
- Appreciation of their bodies

★ THE COMPLETE LEARNING CENTER BOOK

Art Activities

Winter Pictures

3+

Children enhance their winter drawings with Styrofoam.

Words to use

winter
snow
white
Styrofoam

Materials

non-toxic glue
white Styrofoam packing chips
construction paper
crayons, markers

What to do

1. Have children draw a winter background scene—a bare tree, a snowman or a landscape.
2. Provide white Styrofoam packing material and glue.
3. Children glue Styrofoam chips onto their winter scene.

★ THE INSTANT CURRICULUM

Snowflakes

3+

Children learn how to make snowflakes with unusual designs.

Words to use

snowflake
tissue paper
tear
pieces
glue

Materials

metal juice lids (enough for each child in class)
white tissue paper, bond paper or tissues torn in small pieces
glue

What to do

1. Save enough metal juice lids for each child to make one or more snowflakes.
2. Cover the flat side of the juice lid with glue.
3. Ask the children to tear or cut small pieces of paper and put them on top of the glue on the lid.
4. Cover this with glue again and let dry overnight.
5. When it is dry, the "snowflake" easily pops off the lid.
6. Hang the snowflakes all over the room or in the windows.

Want to do more?

These turn into miniature stained glass windows if you use colored tissue paper. You can add powdered tempera paint to the glue and mix the colored glues or add glitter.

★ THE GIANT ENCYCLOPEDIA OF THEME ACTIVITIES

Snow Scenes   3+

Children mold this "snow" to create their own winter scenes.

Words to use

snow
mold
shape
cardboard

Materials

Ivory Snow soap powder
mixing Bowl
rotary egg beater (hand-operated type)
pieces of fairly sturdy, smooth cardboard cut into rounded, irregularly shaped pieces (about 4" x 2-1/2")—one piece per child
pen
spoon
natural objects—small stones or crystals, bits of bark or tiny sticks, tiny hemlock cones, acorns or acorn caps, holly berries or cranberries, tiny bits of evergreen, etc. Sort these into bowls or baskets

What to do

1. Place about one cup of Ivory Snow in the mixing bowl and add about 3/4 cup water. Beat until the mixture holds stiff peaks; do not over beat—it should be about the consistency of whipped cream. This amount should make enough "snow" for 10-12 pieces of cardboard, depending on size. Let the children help with the measuring, pouring and beating.

2. Write each child's name on the underside of his or her cardboard and have the children choose a few objects with which to create their snow scenes. Mound one to two heaping tablespoonfuls of "snow" onto the cardboard base and spread it out a bit, leaving a little cardboard border around the edge.

3. Press the sticks, stones, etc., gently down into the snow, one at a time. Guide the children a bit as to the placement so that they are creating a woodland scene and not just a jumble. For example, a stick becomes a log on which a little red beeswax bird could perch. Then group a bit of evergreen, a stone and a pine cone or acorn around it. The idea is not to see how many things can fit on the cardboard, but to choose a few objects and place them carefully.

4. Let the snow scenes sit undisturbed for one hour, and then the children can take them home. If you have whipped in too much air, they may need to dry overnight (they will have the consistency of marshmallows).

5. Cut a larger cardboard and make a class scene. A small mirror placed in the snow becomes an icy pond, a larger mound of snow is a hill for sledding. Create skaters, children sledding, snowball throwers and snowmen with colored beeswax. You might even fashion a snowman from the snow.

★ EARTHWAYS

Spray Painting Designs in Snow   3+

The children practice fine motor skills as they squeeze the spray bottles. They will also see that colors turn lighter when they are diluted with water as they land on white snow. They will also notice how colors mix to form new colors when the sprayed areas overlap.

Words to use

squeeze
spray
nozzle
splash
aim
colors
pastels
draw

Materials

spray bottles
food coloring, several colors
snow

What to do

1. This activity is best done with one or two children at a time rather than with a larger group.
2. Mix a fairly strong concentration of food coloring into the water in the spray bottles.
3. Outside, let the children spray the bottles onto the snow to make splashes of pastel color on the white snow.
4. Show them how to aim the nozzle away from themselves and the other children Discuss why this is necessary.

Want to do more?

This method can be used to add color to snow sculptures and snow drawings.

★ The Outside Play and Learning Book

Snow Drawings and Prints   3+

Encourage children's creativity by challenging them to think of novel materials to make patterns and designs. The math concept of one-to-one correspondence may be absorbed as the children use one container to make one imprint.

Words to use

imprint
design
guess

Materials

sticks
materials that make an interesting print pattern such as
   juice cans
   potato mashers
   boots
   square containers
   other materials found out-of-doors

What to do

1. Encourage the children to draw pictures or make designs in the snow with the sticks.
2. Embellish the design by making interesting imprint shapes using some of the materials

Want to do more?

Encourage the children to find other objects that would make interesting imprints. See if the children can guess which object made which imprint in the snow. Then they can test their guess by putting the object into the imprint to see if it matches. They could decorate their designs with food coloring spray paint (see Spray Painting Designs in Snow, page 102).

★ The Outside Play and Learning Book

Stuffed Stuff

3+

Think big, really big for this activity.

Words to use

large
big
gigantic

Materials

scraps of butcher paper about 1 yard square
newspaper or other large scrap paper
pens, crayons, paints and brushes
stapler
scissors
yarn

What to do

1. Choose a shape or design such as a fish, pumpkin, animal or abstract shape.
2. Draw it very large on a square of butcher paper.
3. An adult or the artist can cut out the shape from the outline. To make two shapes at once, staple two sheets together and then cut them at the same time. There will be two separate shapes.
4. Paint, draw or otherwise decorate both sides of the shape with colors, or glue additional items on for decoration.
5. Staple the two sheets together at the edge. Leave an opening on one of the sides of the shape.
6. Now stuff the shape with bunched up newspaper or other scraps of paper to fill out the shape. When filled, staple the closing.
7. Add yarn, if desired, to hang the Stuffed Stuff from the ceiling.

Want to do more?

Stuff the shapes with gifts, prizes, candy, rewards or other fun items. Give this project to someone special. Make an entire zoo, undersea world or crazy shape garden out of Stuffed Stuff.

Teaching tips

Young artists love large artwork. The stapling can be difficult, but allow the artist to do as much as possible.

Ice Painting   3+

Challenge children's creativity with this definitely cold material.

Words to use

ice
paint
freeze

Materials

ice tray
popsicle sticks
powdered tempera paint
paper

What to do

1. Put water in an ice tray and stick a popsicle stick in each cubicle
2. Freeze.
3. Sprinkle powdered tempera paint on drawing paper.
4. Encourage children to use the ice cube and stick like a paintbrush.

★ WHERE IS THUMBKIN?

Peanut Collage   3+

A creative use for leftover peanut shells.

Words to use

shells   texture
collage   glue
stick   design
peanut   shape

Materials

peanut shells
glue
drawing paper
scissors, optional

What to do

1. Save peanut shells from a peanut butter making project to create textured collages.
2. If desired, the paper can be cut into the shape of a peanut.

★ WHERE IS THUMBKIN?

Marvelous Mittens

3+

Children use their creativity to make mittens.

Words to use

mitten
decorate
unique

Materials

construction paper
scissors
decorations such as sequins, beads, confetti, tissue paper
glue

What to do

1. Cut mittens from construction paper.
2. Invite the children to decorate a pair of mittens using sequins, beads, confetti, tissue paper, wallpaper scraps or any other scrap materials.

★ WHERE IS THUMBKIN?

Snow Paint

4+

Adding Epsom salts to paint creates wonderful, winter-like surprises.

Words to use

sparkle
crystal
salt
dissolve
brush
paint

Materials

dark construction paper such as purple and blue
crayons
paintbrushes
4 tablespoons Epsom salts
1/4 cup hot water
small cups or bowls
covered table

What to do

1. Mix one-quarter cup hot water with four tablespoons of Epsom salts. Stir mixture to dissolve.
2. Draw freely with crayons on the dark construction paper.
3. Brush the drawing with the salt mixture.
4. Dry the painting completely.

Want to do more?

Cut snowy designs from the paper and hang with string.

Teaching tips

The salt will dry to a snowy, crystal effect. Stir the salt water each time a brush is dipped into the container to keep the brush full of very salty water. The salt crystals brush off the paper when dry. Table salt or rock salt can substitute for Epsom salts.

★ PRESCHOOL ART

Blizzards   4+

Learn how to make a "blizzard" with this activity.

Words to use

blizzard
blow
glitter

Materials

baby food jars and lids
hot glue gun and glue sticks
small figures to put in jar
confetti, glitter or Styrofoam pellets
water

What to do

1. Assemble all the materials and work one-on-one with the children.
2. Heat the glue gun. Always use caution when using the glue gun with children.
3. The child selects the materials he needs.
4. The teacher glues the figure to the inside of the jar lid.
5. Fill the jar almost to the top with the water.
6. Add the glitter or other snow-like filler.
7. Screw the lid on tightly.
8. Turn the jar over so the lid is on the bottom.
9. Shake the jar and watch the blizzard!

★ THEMESTORMING

Finger Knitting

Children practice fine motor skills while making a usable material.

Words to use

yarn   knit

rope   coil

Materials

bulky wool yarn

scissors

a basket or cloth sack for each child's work

What to do

1. Ask at your local yarn shop for 100% wool, bulky weight yarn. Don't forget to ask for a teachers discount! Try to get real wool rather than acrylic, as the wool comes from nature and has a much nicer, warmer feel. It's much more pleasant to work with. The younger the children, the thicker the yarn should be. You could also use cotton yarn, but it is often not as thick and tends not to slide as easily.

2. Cut long lengths of yarn (four to five foot lengths), and have the children roll them into balls. Give each child a small handwork basket or cloth sack marked with his or her name in which the projects "in process" can be kept. This keeps the materials organized and lets the children work on the projects for days at a time.

3. Start the finger knitting by making a slip knot. Lay one end of the yarn across your open palm and hold the end down with your thumb. Wrap the yarn once around your fingers and cross over the first piece. Hold it down again at the crossing point with your thumb. Now you have a loop around your fingers. Still holding on with your thumb, slide the loop off your fingers. Bring the long side of the yarn back through this loop to make a second loop, and while still holding the short end of the yarn, pull the second loop up. This will make a knot by tightening the first loop. If the second loop gets too long and unwieldy, just pull on the long "tail" of the loop to make it smaller.

4. Continue finger knitting by reaching down through the loop to pull the yarn strand up through the loop. Always hold the finger-knitted strand firmly and near the open loop.

Note: It's nice to have a little verse to help the children remember what to do. Here's a suggestion:

> *Reach into the lake, (The open loop)*
> *Catch a fish to bake. (Pull up the yarn)*

5. When you get close to the end of the yarn, pull the end up through the loop to knot it off.

6. If you have a particular finished length in mind, start finger knitting with approximately four to five times that length.

7. The resulting knit "ropes" can be used for free play in many different ways. We kept a basket full of them on our shelf, and they were used for horse reins (place the center of the rope at the back of the neck, bring the two ends to the front, cross the ends and bring them under the armpits to the back); hoses for fire fighters; ties for cloth capes and other clothing; for "wrapping" presents; for building houses, making gates, etc. They are very useful.

8. You can also use the finger knitting to make more conventional items. They make perfect mitten strings. Stitch one end to each one of a pair of mittens or gloves. Run the string through the child's coat sleeves—no more lost mittens! A very nice rug can be made by coiling the finger knitting and stitching it together to make a round braided-type rug. Perhaps your playhouse or doll houses could use one. Or you could be very ambitious and make one for your story corner.

★ EARTHWAYS

Snowy Etching
5+

Children discover the mystery of uncovering hidden layers of color.

Words to use

scratch   design
layers   colors

Materials

crayons
white drawing paper, any size
scraping tool such as blunt pencil, scissors
   point, paper clip or spoon

What to do

1. Using muscles and determination, completely color a piece (or section) of white drawing paper. Color hard and shiny using various colors of blue, white and gray crayons.

2. Using black or dark blue, color over the first layer of colors.

3. When complete, scratch a design of a snowman, a snowy day, snowflakes or any other design into the top layer of crayon. The first layer will show through.

Want to do more?

Instead of a second layer of crayon, use white or black paint over the first layer of crayon. Then fingerpaint in the paint. The slick, shiny crayon background will act like fingerpainting paper. Color a square, circle or other shape in the center of the paper, reducing the challenge of coloring such a large area.

Teaching tips

Smooth matte board instead of paper works very well in this project. Paper can sometimes wrinkle and tear with vigorous coloring. This activity is recommended for artists with enough patience and muscular strength to color a thick layer over a full sheet of paper. Not all artists should be expected to work at this pace or intensity.

★ PRESCHOOL ART

Paste Batik   5+

Discover many wonderful designs with this paste.

Words to use

paste
batik
design

Materials

1/2 cup flour
1/2 cup water
2 teaspoons alum
tape
water
scissors
blender
iron
small piece of 100% cotton
    muslin, unlaundered
corrugated cardboard
several squeeze bottles
paste food color from cake decorating store
several clean, empty shallow cans
paintbrushes

What to do

1. Mix the first three ingredients into a paste using a blender. Put some of the paste in several squeeze bottles.
2. Tape the muslin square to a square of cardboard. Draw with the squeeze bottles of paste on the muslin. Try to maintain a smooth flow of paste. Dots, lines and solid masses are also effective. Dry the project overnight.
3. Mix paste food colors in shallow tin cans with water. A small amount will give a rich hue.
4. Dip paintbrush into the food color mixture and brush colors over the entire piece of muslin, including over the paste design. Dry the project completely.
5. Chip and rub the dry paste off the muslin with fingers. The drawing underneath will be white.

Want to do more?

Make a greeting card by gluing the batik to a piece of colored paper.

Teaching tips

Shallow tuna or pineapple cans are more stable than tall containers for the paste food coloring. A large three by five foot piece of muslin would work for a group project.

★ Preschool Art

Salt Figurines   5+

Sculpt with snow outside and then inside with this mixture.

Words to use

ceramic clay
mold
sculpt

Materials

salt ceramic clay mixture: one cup salt, 1/2 cup cornstarch, 3/4 cup water
saucepan and wooden spoon
stove
cardboard tube or empty frozen juice can
toothpicks
decorating materials such as yarn, feathers, cotton, fabric trims, felt, lace, colored paper, scraps
    of fabric
glue or tape

What to do

1. With adult help, cook the clay ingredients over medium heat in a saucepan. Stir with a wooden spoon until the mixture thickens into a ball. Remove from heat and place on a piece of foil to cool. Knead the dough thoroughly.
2. Fill the tube with clay or something else heavy enough to keep it from tipping over.
3. Place a ball of clay on top of the tube for head. Add other bits of colored clay for facial features. If features won't stick, moisten the clay with a bit of water and then attach. Toothpicks also help features stick to the clay.
4. Dry for several days until the heads and tube fillings are dry.
5. Add any decorations for clothing, hair, hats, glasses, beards, arms or braids. Use glue or tape.

Teaching tips

Salt Ceramic clay often needs to be re-kneaded to make it smooth and pliable again. Clay can be stored in an airtight plastic bag until ready to use. Salt ceramic dries to a rock hardness without being baked.

★ Preschool Art

Circle Time and Group Activities

Five Little Snowmen Fat

3+

Children learn fine motor skills, beginning counting skills and about activities to do in the snow.

Words to use

fingers   hat
head   sun
snowman

Materials

What to do

1. During circle time talk about all the things you can do in the snow, such as sledding, ice skating, building snowmen.
2. Talk about how to make a snowman. Ask the children if they have helped build a snowman. Talk about why snow melts.
3. Show the children the motions for the following fingerplay.

    Five Little Snowmen

    Five little snowmen fat (hold up five fingers and then hold arms out in front
    * like a snowman)*
    Each with a funny hat. (hold hands on top of head to represent hat)
    Out came the sun and melted one. (hold arms above head to represent sun)
    What a sad thing was that. (make a sad face)
    Down, down, down. (move hands down each time down is said)
    Four little snowmen fat....(hold up four fingers)
    Three little snowmen fat....(hold up three fingers)
    Two little snowmen fat....(hold up two fingers)
    One little snowman fat....(hold up one finger)

4. Ask the children to say the words and do the motions with you.

Want to do more?

Art and Math: Make a snowman puppet. Children cut three different sized circles from white construction paper. Glue the circles together from largest to smallest (seriation). Decorate face with markers and glue a tongue depressor to the back.

Large motor: After a snowfall, go outside and build a snowman or make snow angels.

Books to read

Geraldine's Big Snow by Holly Keller
Our Snowman by M.B. Goffstein
Sadie and the Snowman by Allen Morgan
Snow by Kathleen Todd
The Snowman by Raymond Briggs

Let's Go Ice Skating   3+

Children learn about ice freezing and how materials can "skate" across the ice.

Words to use

ice
freeze
skate

Materials

small bowls, such as margarine tubs (1 per child)
1 large shallow container
water
small plastic people (1 per child)

What to do

1. In advance, fill containers halfway with water and freeze.
2. At circle time show the children the containers of ice and ask them to describe the ice (cold, smooth, slippery).
3. Ask the children to gather around the large container. Show the children how to slide the plastic people across the ice in the container. Talk about ice skating and how children would dress if they were going ice skating.
4. Give the children each a bowl and a plastic person to pretend to skate across the ice.

Want to do more?

Dramatic play: Provide mittens for the children to wear during pretend snow play.
Field trip: Take a field trip to a skating rink.
Science: Allow the ice to melt and make periodic observations during the day, talking about the ice melting.

Book to read

Ice Is...Wheee! by Carol Greene

circle time activities...

Snowfolks

Children learn how sun melts the snow.

Words to use

snow
melt
poem
verse

Materials

construction paper
patterns for snowfolks
    and the sun
paper towels
glue
flannel board

What to do

1. In advance, cut the
   outlines of five snow-
   folks and the sun out
   of construction paper
   and glue the outlines
   to paper towels (to
   provide a surface that will adhere to the flannel board).

2. At circle time place the five snowfolks on the flannel board and tell the children a story about the
   snowfolks.

3. Remove the number of snowfolks according to the words of the following poem.

> *Snowfolks*
>
> *Five people made of snow.*
> *Five snowfolks in a row.*
> *They like to feel the cold wind blow, wsh-wsh. (blow into cupped hands)*
> *Bright sun shines down one day. (hold hands over head)*
> *One snow child melts away.*
> *Now there are four left in the row.*
>
> *Four people made of snow.*
> *Four snowfolks in a row.*
> *They like to feel the cold wind blow, wsh-wsh. (blow into cupped hands)*
> *Bright sun shines down one day. (hold hands over head)*
> *One snow girl melts away.*
> *Now there are three left in the row.*

Three people made of snow.
Three snowfolks in a row.
They like to feel the cold wind blow, wsh-wsh. (blow into cupped hands)
Bright sun shines down one day. (hold hands over head)
One snow boy melts away.
Now there are two left in the row.

Two people made of snow.
Two snowfolks in a row.
Bright sun shines down one day
Both snowfolks melt away.
Now there are none left in the row.

Song to sing

"Five Green Speckled Frogs"

★ THE GIANT ENCYCLOPEDIA OF CIRCLE TIME AND GROUP ACTIVITIES

Snowman, Snowman   3+

Children learn about shapes and how a snowman is made.

Words to use

round	ball
pack	shape
snowman	eyes
mouth	arms
body	fat
melt	nose

Materials

picture of snowman

What to do

1. At circle time, show the children a picture of a snowman and talk about how a snowman is made.
2. Ask the children the following questions: What shape is his body, round or square? What kind of eyes, nose, mouth, arms does he have?
3. Ask the children to pretend to make a snowman or snowwoman using their hands to pack the snow.
4. Ask the children what will happen when the sun shines on the snow.

5. Tell the children to pretend to be snowmen or snowwomen and to follow you in acting out the words of the song.

"Snowman, Snowman" (Tune: "Twinkle, Twinkle, Little Star")

Snowman, snowman where did you go?
I built you yesterday out of snow.
I built you round, I built you fat. (make body look fat)
I love you and that is that.
But the sun melted you away. (slowly lower body to the floor)
Good-bye for now, I guess I'll play.

Want to do more?

Art: Make a paper bag snowman or snowwoman. Stuff small, medium and large paper bags with newspaper. Paint the bags white and tape the bags together. Add facial features and a hat.
Outdoors: If there is snow, make a snowman as a class project.
Science: Conduct a melting experiment. Place the same number of ice cubes in the sun and the shade. Periodically observe the ice cubes and record your observations.

★ The Giant Encyclopedia of Circle Time and Group Activities

What Can You Do in Winter Time?   3+

Children, even those who live in warm climates, learn about things to do in cold, snowy weather.

Words to use

winter
cold
warm
coats
hot chocolate
covers
shiver
mittens
scarves
hats

Materials

pictures of winter activities and snow

What to do

1. At circle time show the children the pictures of winter activities and show and talk about the kinds of activities children can do in the winter.
2. Sing the following song to the children and explain that you will ask them to suggest ways to keep warm and you will add their suggestions to the song.

"What Can We Do in Winter Time?" (Tune: "Muffin Man")

What can we do in the winter time, the winter time, the winter time?
Oh, what can we do in the winter time
To keep ourselves warm?

3. Ask children to suggest a way, such as wear a coat.

Children put your coats on
Children put your coats on
Children put your coats on to keep yourselves warm.

4. Make up additional verses adding the children's suggestions, such as drink hot chocolate, get under the covers.

Want to do more?

Math: Provide a basket of summer and winter clothes and ask the children to sort the clothing into a summer pile and a winter pile. Ask the children the kind of fasteners they have on their coats and make a graph comparing the number of coats that have zippers, buttons, Velcro.

★ THE GIANT ENCYCLOPEDIA OF CIRCLE TIME AND GROUP ACTIVITIES

The Snowman 3+

Teaches children sequencing skills.

Words to use

big	round
snowball	roll
scarf	buttons
hat	

Materials

What to do

Ask the children to pretend to be snowmen, first by growing tall and then by slowly melting away.

I made a little snowman,
I made him big and round.
I made him from a snowball,
I rolled upon the ground.
He has two eyes, a nose, a mouth,
A lovely scarf of red.
He even has some buttons,
And a hat upon his head.
Melt, melt, melt, melt,
Melt, melt, melt, melt.

★ 500 FIVE MINUTE GAMES

Winter Wind

3+

Children learn about the wind.

Words to use

wind
blow
strong
gentle

Materials

candles
matches
books
feathers

What to do

1. Call a Learning Circle to talk about the wind.
2. Some questions to ask about the wind are:

> *What is wind?*
> *Where does the wind come from?*
> *Can we see the wind?*
> *When does the wind help us?*
> *When is the wind harmful?*
> *When the wind leaves, where does it go?*

3. Ask each child to blow forcefully in the palm of their hand. Feel the wind!
4. Let each child blow out a candle. (The teacher lights the candle.) The wind can be very strong. It can blow over trees and telephone poles!
5. Ask each child to blow on a book.
6. Next, each child blows on a feather. Imagine a bird soaring on the wind using its feathers.

Want to do more?

Use a hair dryer to demonstrate the effect that wind has on different objects. Use it on a feather, a scarf, a sock, a marble and a paper cup. Some objects will roll, some are lifted up in the air, some need a stronger wind to move them and some bounce.

★ THE LEARNING CIRCLE

Cold Talk

Understanding the concept of cold is important to understanding winter weather.

Words to use

cold
ice cube
melt

Materials

ice cubes
bowls

What to do

1. In advance, make ice cubes. Give each child a bowl with ice cubes in it.
2. Tell them that they may feel the ice while discussing the cold questions.
3. Feeling the sensation of cold will intensify the experience.
4. Suggested questions are:
   - ✓ How do you feel when you are cold?
   - ✓ What feels cold when you touch it?
   - ✓ When you feel cold, what can you do to feel warm?
   - ✓ What do animals do when they feel cold?
   - ✓ Would you rather feel hot or cold?

Want to do more?

Act out some cold imagination games. Imagine walking barefoot in the snow or building an imaginary snowman. Push the snow together and round it out. Lift the body sections. Hunt for berries to make the buttons. Stand back and admire the snowman. Go camping. Set up a tent. Unfold the sleeping bags and climb in. Zip up. It's a cold night!

Teaching tips

During the Cold Talk activity, a cold weather puppet such as a polar bear or penguin can ask the questions. Wear mittens and rub your hands briskly at the start of a new question. Have everyone rub their hands together until a volunteer is chosen to answer.

★ THE LEARNING CIRCLE

C-C-C-C-Cold

3+

Develops children's weather vocabulary.

Words to use

sing   cold
north   shiver

Materials

What to do

1. Recite the following call and response chant.
2. When the children say the c-c-c-c-cold line, they cross their arms over their chests and pretend to shiver.

> *There was a man and he did sing,*
> *C-c-c-c-cold.*
> *Across the north land it would ring,*
> *C-c-c-c-cold.*
> *No matter what he tried to say,*
> *C-c-c-c-cold.*
> *His words kept coming out this way,*
> *C-c-c-c-cold.*

3. This song is an excellent introduction to a discussion of proper clothing for cold weather.

★ 500 FIVE MINUTE GAMES

Hungry Bunny

3+

This poem encourages children's creativity while developing their coordination.

Words to use

carrot
nose
bunny
hungry

Materials

carrot sticks

What to do?

1. This is a nice poem to act out on a cold winter day.

> *A funny little snowman*
> *Had a carrot nose.*
> *Along came a bunny,*
> *And what do you suppose?*
> *That bunny was very hungry*
> *And was looking for some lunch.*
> *He ate that little snowman's nose,*
> *Crunch, crunch, crunch.*

2. Let the children take turns being the bunny and the snowman.
3. Pass out carrots for the children to eat at the sound of "crunch."

★ 500 FIVE MINUTE GAMES

Mushy, Slushy, Melty Snow   4+

Gaining an awareness of the different forms that water takes is a part of every child's science learning. This activity uses snow, a modified form of water, and asks children to change it from the solid form to the liquid.

Words to use

melt	energy
cold	heat
shake	water
liquid	solid
change	snow
ice	slush

Materials

baby food jars with lids or clear plastic containers with lids for each child
snow—if no snow is available, use crushed ice or slush made in a blender

What to do

1. Bring in and have stored in a cold place the baby food jars half full of packed snow. A smaller amount will melt faster, something you may want to consider in planning.
2. Discuss what happens to snow when it is brought inside. Show how water is formed when this material melts in your hands. The heat from your hand causes the snow to melt.
3. Give each child a container with snow and ask them to help the snow to melt. How can they make the jar warmer so the snow melts faster? They can use their hands, breathe on it, put it under their shirts or anything else they can come up with. Just be sure that the lids stay on tight.
4. As the snow melts in containers, discuss what conditions are best for melting snow. Use the terms liquid, melt, cold and heat, regarding the snow changing to water. One discovery you will make is that "the more heat applied, the faster it will melt." Another discovery will be that mixing the snow by shaking occasionally will hurry the melting process. Asking the children to describe how they made their snow melt will help the group discover these facts for themselves.

Want to do more?

Use a thermometer to note temperature changes as the snow heats up and melts. Change the water back into a solid by refreezing it and compare it to the original snow. How many words can you think of to describe snow, ice and water?

★ MUDPIES TO MAGNETS

The Star Seat   4+

This activity provides a special moment of affirmation for a child. Choosing the right time and child is important.

Words to use

appreciate   cheer
encourage   special

Materials

sheet of felt to drape over the back of a chair
stars of different sizes cut from yellow felt
assorted decorations
white glue
small chair

What to do

1. Drape the felt sheet across the art table and set out decorations and glue. Tell the children that you need their help to make a blanket for a Star Seat. Invite them to glue the various stars and decorations onto the felt blanket.
2. When the blanket has been completed and the glue completely dried, bring it to circle time. Drape it over the back of a small chair next to you. Tell the children that this is a Star Seat.
3. Ask for a volunteer to sit in the Star Seat. After the special person sits in the chair, mention some of the things you appreciate about that person. Invite other children to do likewise. Tell the group that you want them to cheer and clap when the person in the Star Seat gives his name. Ask the volunteer his name and start cheering. Raise your hands when you want the cheering to stop.
4. Conduct no more than two Star Seat cheers during a single circle time. Be sure to give every child an opportunity over a period of time.

Want to do more?

If a child makes a negative comment about someone in the Star Seat, respond with, "Yes, that upsets you when (child's name) does that. Right now we are thinking about the things we appreciate about (child's name)."

★ THE PEACEFUL CLASSROOM

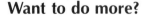

Dramatic Play Activities

Ambulance for Emergency Care

3+

This activity encourages the development of social skills and helps children understand how ambulances help people.

Words to use

ambulance
siren
help
hurt
injury
sound
loud
hurry
hospital

Materials

child's wagon
pillows
plastic container or cup
paper
tape
markers

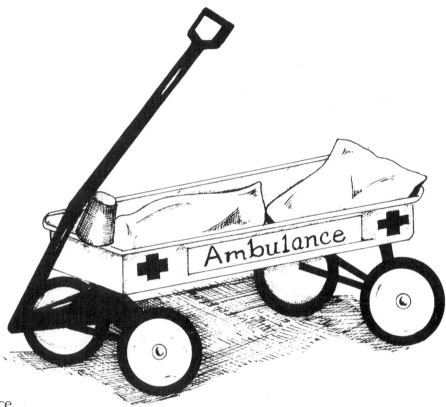

What to do

1. Use a child's wagon as the frame for the ambulance
2. Place pillows inside the wagon.
3. Make a siren from a plastic container or cup.
4. Decorate the ambulance to look like those used in the area.
5. Discuss the design and sound of the ambulances the children have seen.

★ THE COMPLETE LEARNING CENTER BOOK

The Librarian   3+

Sharing this book helps children to understand the role of a librarian and how to use this information as they "pretend" in the Library Center.

Words to use

librarian
books
help
read

Materials

Librarians A to Z by Jean Johnson, or any other books about librarians or libraries

What to do

1. Discuss the responsibilities of the workers in the library after reading *Librarians A to Z*.
2. This book includes pictures of a librarian working and interacting with young children.

★ THE COMPLETE LEARNING CENTER BOOK

Medical Charting   3+

Children learn to measure and distinguish alike and different shapes, important math skills.

Words to use

chart
height
tall
mark
measure

Materials

large sheet of paper
tape
markers
construction paper

What to do

1. Tape a large piece of paper on the wall of the doctor's office center.
2. Two children work together, one child stands and the other marks his or her height.
3. Make hand or foot prints on smaller pieces of paper.
4. Compare, contrast and group the prints.

★ THE COMPLETE LEARNING CENTER BOOK

Don't Move—Help Is on the Way

This activity provides an opportunity to talk about what to do when people get injured. If you play the role of one of the "paramedics," you could ask the other "paramedic" what he thinks should be done and suggest treatments based on described symptoms.

Words to use

accident
victim
help
ambulance
doctor

Materials

a wagon
a tricycle decorated with a red cross
a doctor kit
doctor and nurse hats
white jackets (use old shirts)
long strips of white fabric (an old sheet torn up) for bandages
a telephone

What to do

1. First you need a victim or victims at the scene of the "accident" or "fire."
2. You could attach a wagon to the ambulance tricycle, and the "paramedics" could give first aid and then haul the victim to the "hospital."

Want to do more?

Create a "hospital" to receive victims. A cardboard box could be opened and spread out on the ground for a bed. A box or shelf will be needed for medical supplies. Various "doctor" supplies, such as a stethoscope, rubber gloves, bottles, cotton balls and a clip board with paper and pencil will be useful.

★ THE OUTSIDE PLAY AND LEARNING BOOK

JANUARY

dramatic play activities

Language Activities

What Is It?   3+

This activity challenges children's observation skills and their imagination.

Words to use

light
move
shadows
describe

Materials

high intensity lamp or projector light
sheet

What to do

1. Place a sheet on the wall or use a movie screen.
2. Create a light source by using a high intensity lamp or projector light.
3. Using your hands in between the light source and the screen, make shadows on the screen with your hands and let children describe what they "see."

★ THE INSTANT CURRICULUM

Recipe Collection   3+

Children learn sequencing skills and vocabulary development.

Words to use

favorite
sandwich
collection

Materials

paper and pencil or pen

What to do

1. Ask children to dictate their recipes for their favorite sandwich.
2. Transcribe their dictation onto paper, creating a class recipe book. (This will be a humorous collection, one that parents will love!)

★ WHERE IS THUMBKIN?

Footprint Concentration   3+

This activity enhances children's visual memory skills.

Words to use

footprint
fox
duck
chicken
match
just like
same as
different from
set

★ make two of each footprint card

Materials

index cards
markers and crayons

What to do

1. Draw animal footprints on the index cards. Make two fox footprint cards, two ducks and two chickens.
2. The children turn the cards face down.
3. They take turns trying to turn up a matched set.

★ WHERE IS THUMBKIN?

Flannel Board Stories

These story boards are a wonderful way for children to share stories with friends and parents. These retelling experiences increase the child's comprehension of the story while building confidence in language abilities.

Words to use

book
story
retell
flannel board

Materials

stiff paper
crayons and markers
scissors
glue
sandpaper or felt
flannel board
flannel and cardboard
labeled plastic bags

What to do

1. Ask the children to choose their favorite books in the Library Center.
2. Use these stories to make flannel board presentations.
3. Ask the children, in small groups or individually, to draw the characters, scenery or props that are needed to tell the story.
4. Use stiff paper for the drawings, with small pieces of coarse sandpaper or felt glued on the back of the characters and scenery to make them adhere to the flannel board.
5. Let the children tell the story using the props they have created.
6. Place these and other flannel stories in plastic bags with labels and store them in the Library Center.
7. Encourage the children to take a story home to share with their parents.
8. Construct small portable flannel boards by taping inexpensive flannel to cardboard.

① draw on felt with marker

② cut out

③ glue coarse sandpaper or felt pieces to back of characters

★ THE COMPLETE LEARNING CENTER BOOK

language activities

A Story Box

Children enjoy repeating the gingerbread boy's chant as the story is told.

Words to use

story
chant
tell
flannel board
felt
props story box

Materials

school box or cigar box
felt scraps
fabric glue or glue gun
scissors
wiggly eyes

cover inside lid with felt to make a flannel board

What to do

1. In advance, cover the inside lid of the school box with felt to make a flannel board. Cut out the gingerbread boy and the other characters from felt using the illustrated patterns. (Enlarge patterns as needed.) Glue on the eyes, mouths and other details. Store the pieces in the box.
2. Tell the children that they can help you make some gingerbread cookies.
3. First they will need to get out a big bowl. (Pretend to hold a bowl.)
4. Next, let the children suggest different ingredients to put in the cookies. (Pretend to put these in and mix up the dough.)
5. Have the children pretend to roll out the dough and cut out a gingerbread boy.
6. Open the story box, and tell the traditional story of the gingerbread boy using the props in the story box.
7. Encourage the children to say the following lines of the story with you:

> *"Run, run, fast as you can.*
> *You can't catch me, 'cause I'm the gingerbread man!"*

Want to do more?

Let the children act out the story. Make gingerbread cookies for snack. Make other flannel board story boxes.

★ TRANSITION TIME

JANUARY

language activities

Storytelling Together

3+

Builds children's creative thinking.

Words to use

objects   sentence
repeat   story

Materials

bag
assorted objects

What to do

1. Place several objects inside a bag.
2. Ask one child to pick out an object and say one sentence about it. Help him if needed.
3. For example, if the object is a ball, suggest he say, "Once upon a time, there was a ball."
4. Ask another child a question about the ball. For example, "Where does the ball live?"
5. After she answers, repeat the story they have created so far. "Once upon a time there was a ball, and it lived in the toy box."
6. Continue the story by adding new objects from the bag.

★ 500 FIVE MINUTE GAMES

Book Buddies

3+

This activity helps children learn to share.

Words to use

buddy
friend

Materials

stuffed animals
variety of books such as big books, little books; books from the library; books children bring from
    home; homemade books
bookshelf

What to do

1. Make an attractive display with books and animals.
2. When the children are through with an activity or want something quiet to do, invite them to get a book and stuffed animal and "read" the book to their animal friend.
3. Encourage the children to tell you about the book.

Want to do more?

Let the children look at books with friends at other in-between times during the day.

JANUARY

language activities

Word Sharing

Builds children's memory and vocabulary skills.

Words to use

remind
related to
remember

Materials

What to do

1. Pick a word that the children know.
2. If you have recently taken a field trip, try using a word that will remind them of the trip.
3. For example, use the word "snow" and ask the children to suggest words related to it.
4. Encourage them to name things to do in the snow.
5. As they talk about the snow, expand their thinking by suggesting a different kind of snow or winter word.
6. For example, ask about sounds they might associate with snow.
7. This game can be simple or complicated to play.

★ 500 FIVE MINUTE GAMES

Interesting Talk

3+

Encourages children to practice their language skills.

Words to use

finish
sentence

Materials

What to do

1. Explain to the children that you would like them to finish a sentence.
2. Begin by saying, "My favorite place to visit is the park because...."
3. Ask them to think about why the park is a favorite place.
4. Begin other sentences for the children to finish.
5. Younger children may have difficulty with this game. Try stimulating and building their vocabulary in advance. Then try the game again.

★ 500 FIVE MINUTE GAMES

language activities

Math Activities

How Many Objects Fit on the Paper?   3+

Children learn to arrange objects by the amount of space and to match colors.

Words to use

color
same
fill

Materials

construction paper in primary and secondary colors
assortment of objects of the same color from around the classroom

What to do

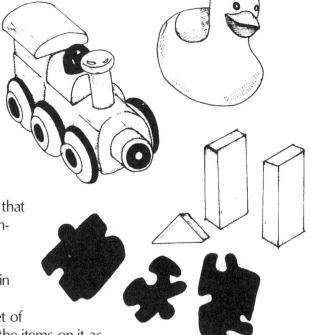

1. Collect items from around the classroom that are primary or secondary colors. For example, puzzle pieces, unifix cubes, wooden counting blocks, toys.
2. Place the items in the center of the table in the mathematics and manipulative area.
3. Have each child at the table select a sheet of construction paper, then put as many of the items on it as he can fit.
4. After each child's paper is filled, have him count the number of items on his paper.

Teaching tips

For young children who do not yet know how to count or who cannot count as high as the number of objects on the paper, count with them as they remove each item from the paper to the table. Have older children compare whether there are more or fewer objects of each color. For example, are there more or fewer purple items than red ones?

★ MORE STORY S-T-R-E-T-C-H-E-R-S

Patterns   3+

Children learn about patterns, how to create them and repeat them.

Words to use

clothespins
paper plate
circular pattern

Materials

forty clothespins
red, yellow, green and blue spray paint
paper plates

What to do

1. Spray paint the clothespins (10 of each color).
Note: Be sure to use the spray paint outside or in a well-ventilated room.
2. Give the children paper plates and clothespins. Ask them to create color patterns. Remind the children that using a clothespin requires using "thumbkin" and "pointer."
3. Encourage the children to create a circular pattern.

★ WHERE IS THUMBKIN?

Big and Little Mittens   3+

Children increase their visual discrimination of objects

Words to use

big
little
pairs

Materials

construction paper
scissors
stapler

What to do

1. Cut several pairs of mittens from construction paper in two different sizes (one small pair, one much larger).
2. Staple the pairs together.
3. Encourage the children to sort the mittens into large and small pairs.

★ WHERE IS THUMBKIN?

Mitten Match

3+

Children learn to recognize similar and different objects.

Words to use

match
the same
pattern
pair

Materials

old wallpaper sample book
scissors
marker
yarn
two thumbtacks
20 spring-type clothespins

What to do

1. Cut a matching pair of mittens from patterned wallpaper. Make a total of ten pairs, each pair from a different pattern of wallpaper.
2. Make a clothesline on the wall using yarn and thumbtacks.
3. The children match the mitten pairs.
4. When a match is made, the children clip them to the line with clothespins.

Want to do more?

Encourage children to match paper mittens by letters, numbers or shapes.

Book to read

The Three Little Kittens by Paul Galdone

★ THE GIANT ENCYCLOPEDIA OF THEME ACTIVITIES

How Deep Is Your Snow Drift?

3+

The purpose of this activity is to observe the depth of snow over a period of time and thereby to recognize the effects of different kinds of weather, such as cold and warm spells, wind and additional snow storms. It is a simple way of recognizing changes that often go unnoticed.

Words to use

snow	freezing
melt	observe
measure	mark
depth	snow storm

Materials

stick
permanent marker
calendar

What to do

1. Before the first snow, place sticks in spots where they can be easily observed and will not be in the way.
2. After the first snow, go out and mark the depth.
3. After a few days or hours, depending on the weather, measure and mark the depth again.
4. After each temperature change or snow storm, measure and mark the depth and date it.
5. When the snow has gone, note the different depths that you have marked for your snow field.

Want to do more?

Make paper snowflakes. Compare snowdrifts in various spots, for instance a windy spot and a quiet spot. Do your measuring with a meter stick. Discuss how snow forms. Ten inches of snow equal one inch of water. How much moisture did your snow provide? Melt snow. Find temperatures on various days at various spots. Record weather conditions on a calendar, along with changes in snow depth. Observe weather conditions and try to predict the effects on the depth of the snow.

★ Hug a Tree

Horizontal Bar Graphs of Birds at Our Winter Feeder

3+

Children help record, count and chart the number of birds they see.

Words to use

bird watching
feeder
unifix cubes
graph
observe

Materials

bird feeder and bird seed
two note pads
pencils
chart tablet or poster
  board
marker
unifix cubes or small
  blocks of same size

Birds at our Winter feeder

Friday	■		
Thursday	■	▨	
Wednesday	■	▨	
Tuesday	■		
Monday	■	▨	▨

What to do

1. Select two bird watchers. Have one child go to the window and look for birds at the feeder at the end of circle time each day. Have the second child look for birds at the end of play or another time each day. Instruct the assigned bird watchers to make a hash mark (/) for each bird they see.
2. Prepare the note pad for the assigned bird watchers by drawing a line down the center of the pages and writing the date at the top of each page of the note pad. The first bird watcher records hash marks on the left and the second bird watcher records hash marks on the right.
3. Prepare a second note pad for incidental observations the other children in the class may make. Date each page of the note pad and ask the children to write their names or initials, then make a hash mark for each bird they see.
4. At the end of the week, make a large bar graph with unifix cubes or colored blocks to show the number of birds the assigned bird watchers saw and the number the other children observed. Place a sheet of chart tablet or poster board on the table. Starting at the bottom of the chart on the left side, write the days of the week, leaving enough space for three unifix cubes. Select three different colors of blocks, a color for each of the two assigned bird watchers and a third color to represent the class observations.
5. Let the children look back at each day's record on the note pad and count the number of birds each of the assigned bird watchers saw and place the same number of unifix cubes or blocks on the chart in a horizontal line across from the date. Count the number of birds the other class members noted and place a corresponding number of blocks on the chart.

Teaching tips

For younger children, prepare a chart representing the class bird watchers. Older children can chart the number of different birds that came to the feeder each day. Older children also can use binoculars to observe the birds.

★ MORE STORY S-T-R-E-T-C-H-E-R-S

Graphing

5+

Helps children develop comparison skills.

Words to use

peanut   shell
compare   graph

Materials

peanuts   graph
marker   stickers

What to do

1. Give each child an unshelled peanut.
2. Have the child open the peanut and count the nuts inside.
3. Make a graph. Let each child illustrate on the graph (make an "x" or place a sticker in the correct square) how many nuts were in his shell.

★ WHERE IS THUMBKIN?

Music and Movement Activities

Movement Clues to Solve Riddles

3+

Children learn to interpret the clues of physical movement to solve a riddle.

Words to use

move
motion
clue

Materials

Is Your Mamma a Llama? by Deborah Guarino

What to do

1. With a small group of children in the library corner, recall all the animals Lloyd, the llama, met in the book *Is Your Mamma a Llama?*
2. Have them think of ways that each animal would move or behave. For example, the bat flies, the swan swims, the cow grazes on grass, the seal swims, the kangaroo hops and the llamas graze, too.
3. After they have decided on the motions, practice them, then have another group of children come over and guess which animals the children are pretending to be by their movement clues.

Teaching tips

If the audience has difficulty deciding on which animal the child is pretending to be, let the child give a clue from the book, such as "My mama lives in a cave."

★ MORE STORY S-T-R-E-T-C-H-E-R-S

Ice Skater's Waltz

3+

Children learn to move like ice skaters.

Words to use

glide
skate
waltz

Materials

Chicken Soup with Rice by Maurice Sendak
tape or record of the "Skater's Waltz" or any waltz music
 and tape or record player
plastic soup bowls

What to do

1. Have the children sit in a circle and take off their shoes so they can glide more easily like ice skaters.
2. Show them the first picture for January in *Chicken Soup with Rice* where the boy is skating while balancing a bowl of hot soup.
3. Start the music and have the children stand in place and sway back and forth to feel the movement of skaters.
4. Give the children empty plastic bowls and ask them to pretend they are skating while sipping hot chicken soup with rice.

Teaching tips

For younger preschoolers, the task of skating and balancing the bowl may be too difficult. Allow them a few practice rounds on the imaginary ice before giving them the bowls. When children do drop their bowls, help them not to feel embarrassed by saying,

> *"It all right, It's so nice,*
> *Now the ice has Chicken soup with rice."*
> *By Shirley Raines*

Undoubtedly, the silly rhyme will produce more pretend spills.

★ STORY S-T-R-E-T-C-H-E-R-S

Mitten, Mitten, Who Has the Mitten?   3+

Children practice how to take turns and learn about sequencing.

Words to use

mitten
lost
animal

Materials

The Mitten by Alvin Tresselt
mitten
lively music on a tape or record
tape or record player
sled or wagon

What to do

1. Have the children seated in a circle on the floor. Place the sled or wagon in the center of the circle.
2. Ask the children to recall the animals from *The Mitten*.
3. Assign each child an animal from the story.
4. For the first turn, you be the little boy who loses his mitten. Start the music and pretend to be picking up firewood and putting it on the sled or in the wagon. Walk in front of a child and accidentally drop the mitten.
5. Stop the music and look all around the wagon or sled for your mitten, then ask, "Mitten, mitten, who has my mitten?"
6. Instead of the child answering, "I do," he must answer with his animal name, "The rabbit has the mitten."
7. The child who has the mitten gets to be the mitten "dropper."

Teaching tips

To avoid some children not being chosen, whisper in the "dropper's" ear the name of the person you want to get the mitten.

★ STORY S-T-R-E-T-C-H-E-R-S

Musical I Spy   3+

Children learn observation skills by describing what they see.

Words to use

move
describe
freeze

Materials

cassette tape or record of light instrumental music
tape or record player

What to do

1. Explain to the children how to play musical "I Spy."
2. When the music begins, they move in any way which the music inspires them. If they can't think of a way to move, they can skip, hop, jump or march, but they must move.

3. When the music stops, they turn around once and freeze, then stare at something straight in front of them.

3. When the music stops, they turn around once and freeze, then stare at something straight in front of them.
4. The teacher then calls on someone and the person says, "I Spy", and describes something she sees.
5. The listeners have three chances to guess what the person spies, then the person tells the answer.
6. The music starts again, and everyone moves however the music makes them feel until the teacher stops the music. Then the process of "I Spy" begins all over again.

Teaching tips

Young children may play "I Spy" by just giving colors and then everyone guesses. There are no winners and losers. The children enjoy moving to the music, freezing when it stops, describing what they see and hoping they will be called on next.

★ STORY S-t-r-e-t-c-h-e-r-s

Relaxing to Music   3+

Children learn to relax while responding to music.

Words to use

messy
pick up
peace

Materials

Five Minutes' Peace by Jill Murphy
record player or cassette tape player
relaxing record or tape

What to do

1. At the end of free play, the housekeeping corner will invariably look like Mrs. Large's house from *Five Minutes' Peace*.
2. Show the children in the housekeeping corner the picture of Mrs. Large's kitchen, and have them put their housekeeping corner back in order while listening to music.
3. At circle time, comment on how the children in the housekeeping corner and the dress-up corner found their house looking like Mrs. Large's until they cleaned it up.

Teaching tips

Children enjoy playing, but often balk when asked to clean up. Regularly scheduled clean-up times, five minutes at the end of free play or learning center time, can alleviate the problem. Establish the clean-up time routine by using the same signal each day, a simple song, "It's clean-up time, It's clean-up time," or a flick of the light switch, or have a child carry around a clean-up time sign for everyone to see. Most importantly, have a routine and keep the same signal each day until clean-up time goes well. Then you can change the signal for variety.

★ STORY S-t-r-e-t-c-h-e-r-s

Balancing Beanbags

Children learn to locate parts of the body in this gross motor activity.

Words to use

parts of the body
beanbag
balance

Materials

one beanbag per child
music for movement with a walking rhythm (record, piano)

What to do

1. Gather children in an open area with room to move.
2. Explain that they will each receive a beanbag and will be moving around the room when the music is playing.
3. As the music plays the teacher names a part of the body for the children to place the beanbag on and try to balance it as they move.

Want to do more?

As children become more adept at balancing and moving, the music can be sped up or varied in rhythm. Children may take turns calling out body parts.

★ THE GIANT ENCYCLOPEDIA OF THEME ACTIVITIES

Bottle Maracas

3+

Children learn how to make their own musical instrument.

Words to use

maracas
rice
shake

Materials

rice or gravel
clear plastic shampoo or detergent bottle
glue

What to do

1. Make a maraca by placing rice or gravel in an empty, clear plastic shampoo or detergent bottle.
2. Glue the lid on for safety.
3. Let children use the maracas as an instrument in the Rhythm Band.

★ THE INSTANT CURRICULUM

JANUARY

music & movement activities

Drums and Sticks 3+

Children learn to make their own musical instruments.

Words to use

drum   stick   rhythm

Materials

empty gallon can with a plastic lid
pencil with eraser or stick with ball of cloth tied to it

What to do

1. Use an empty gallon can with a plastic lid for a simple drum. Children can tap it with the eraser end of pencil or with a stick that has a ball of cloth tied on the end.
2. Dowel sticks may be cut into ten to twelve inch lengths to make rhythm sticks. Wooden kitchen spoons may also be used for the rhythm sticks.
3. Children play the sticks by tapping them on the floor or table or by tapping the sticks together.

★ THE INSTANT CURRICULUM

Color the Movement 4+

Children practice basic movement skills (walking, jumping, hopping, skipping, etc.) with this activity.

Words to use

move
color words

Materials

color strips of construction paper in basic colors such as red, blue, green, orange, purple
recorded music

What to do

1. Cut the strips of paper evenly into large enough pieces (minimum size is 4 x 5-1/2 inches or larger) so they can be readily seen while the children are moving.
2. The children form a circle and the teacher stands in the middle of it.
3. Assign a certain movement to each color (use only two to three colors at first)
4. The teacher plays a recording and asks the children to move as designated by the color shown. For example:
   ✓ green—walk
   ✓ blue—hop
   ✓ yellow—run
5. In order to move smoothly from one movement to another, it may be necessary to designate one color as the "STOP" color. For example:
   ✓ red—stop
   This will prevent chaos or children bumping each other!

Want to do more?

Teacher can divide class into two "teams," each taking turns on a movement as the color is shown. As children become more skilled, the teacher can flash colors more rapidly to determine if children can keep the beat and move smoothly from one basic movement to another.

★ THE GIANT ENCYCLOPEDIA OF THEME ACTIVITIES

Making Horns   4+

Children will enjoy making their own musical instruments and discovering what sounds they can produce.

Words to use

instrument
horn
music

Materials

cardboard tube, one per child
construction paper
crayons or markers
clear contact paper
wax paper
thick rubber bands, one per child
scissors

What to do

1. Give each child a cardboard tube and ask her to choose materials to decorate the outside of it.
2. Cut a piece of clear contact paper large enough to cover the child's design and overlap the lip of the tube.
3. Cut the wax paper 1" larger than the diameter of the end of the tube. Pull wax paper tightly over the end of the tube and secure with a thick rubber band.
4. Use scissors to cut slits in the wax paper and then cut one or two finger holes in the tube itself, near the wax paper end of the tube.
5. Have the children sing or hum "do-do-do, re-re-re..." into the open end of their horns.

Want to do more?

Play follow the leader by repeating the leader's sound. Discuss the feeling of vibration when air is blown into the horn. Discuss different types of sounds the children produce and their qualities.

★ THE GIANT ENCYCLOPEDIA OF THEME ACTIVITIES

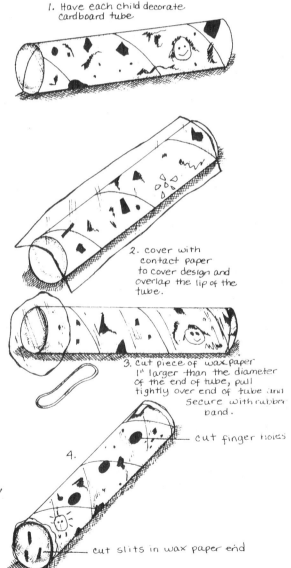

1. Have each child decorate cardboard tube.
2. cover with contact paper to cover design and overlap the lip of the tube.
3. Cut piece of wax paper 1" larger than the diameter of the end of tube, pull tightly over end of tube and secure with rubber band.
4. cut finger holes — cut slits in wax paper end

Science Activities

The Feely Box   **3+**

Children learn how to distinguish materials by the sense of touch only.

Words to use

feel
sock
hide

Materials

empty oatmeal box or coffee can
sock
tape
scissors
assorted items for feeling: block, sponge, spool, sandpaper

What to do

1. Remove the lid from the oatmeal box or coffee can.
2. Tape the top of the sock around the opening of the oatmeal box or coffee can.
3. Cut the toe of the sock off.
4. Place assorted items inside the box or can
5. Invite children to stick their hand through the sock and into the box or can to touch the various items. The children attempt to identify the items by touch only.

★ WHERE IS THUMBKIN?

Bird Pudding   **3+**

Here is a nutritious recipe that birds just love. Children learn measuring skills and that living things need nourishment.

Words to use

suet
fat
food

Materials

electric frying pan or pan and hot plate
wooden spoon
measuring cups
2 cups suet, melted
2 cups sugar
1 cup flour
4 cups cornmeal
margarine tubs, paper cups or citrus fruit rinds
string

What to do

1. Melt the fat (suet), then add all the other ingredients and mix well.
   Note: Use caution with the electric frying pan or hot plate. The fat can spatter. The suet may not melt completely. You can cool and drain the solid pieces that remain, tie them with string and hang them from a tree. Some peanut butter can be used as part of the fat.
2. Pack the mixture in margarine tubs, paper cups, fruit rinds or coconut shells for hanging. Hang them on the treat tree as needed.
3. Extra mixture can be stored in the freezer until you need it.

★ THE OUTSIDE PLAY AND LEARNING BOOK

Tin Can Ice Cream

3+

Ice cream! Ice cream! We all love ice cream. It's even better when you make it yourself, especially if you can taste it as you go along to be sure it's just right.

Words to use

freeze   mixture
mix   ice cream
flavor

Materials

soda pop or beer cans (wash thoroughly and remove the tops, leaving no sharp edges)
snow or crushed ice
tongue depressors or popsicle sticks
milk
flavoring
large plastic cottage cheese or deli containers from the supermarket
sugar
canned milk (evaporated)
spoons

What to do

1. Select a can for each child. Aluminum cans let the ice cream freeze faster, but soup cans will work too.
2. Select a plastic container for each child. Place some salt in the bottom of it.
3. Place the cans in the plastic containers.
4. Layer snow and more salt into the plastic containers until the snow is high on the sides of the cans.
5. Pour 1/2 cup milk into each can.
6. Add 1 tablespoon each of sugar and canned milk.
7. If flavoring is desired, add your favorite, i.e. vanilla, chocolate or other extracts.
8. Stir the mixture with the wooden tongue depressor. They key here is to scrape the freezing ice cream away from the sides of the can so that more milk can be frozen.
9. When the mixture has reached the consistency of a thick shake, it's ready to eat. This takes about 10 minutes. Add more salt to the snow if it's taking too long. Tasting makes the time go quickly!

Want to do more?

Add fruit and nuts to the mixture. Use thermometers to check the temperature of the snow, the snow and salt, and the milk mixture. Measure the amount of salt added to the mixture to change freezing time. For those who can't have milk, freeze juices. Another approach is to place a small covered jar of the ice cream mixture in the middle of a coffee can filled with snow and salt. Put a lid on the can. Shake the can until the ice cream is frozen.

★ HUG A TREE

Catch the Falling Snow   3+

Children learn about the properties of snow.

Words to use

snow
melt
designs

Materials

shallow pan
falling snow

What to do

1. Set a shallow pan outside on a snowy day to catch the falling snow. Bring the pan inside and watch the snow melt into water.
2. Catch snowflakes on dark construction paper

★ 500 FIVE MINUTE GAMES

Ice Castles

3+

Children observe and experiment with the scientific principles of freezing and melting.

Words to use

freeze
ice
castle
melt
create
shapes
tall
short

Materials

one plastic container for each child (the more different sizes and shapes of containers, the more interesting the castle will look)
masking tape and permanent marker
water
pitcher
food coloring

What to do

1. Put the water in a pitcher. Label the containers with the children's names. Have each child pour water into his container (leaving room at the top for the water to expand).
2. Have each child put one or two drops of food coloring into the water.
3. Put the containers outside overnight to freeze (use a freezer if the weather isn't cold enough).
4. The next day pop the frozen creations out of their containers. Place them outside on a flat surface next to one another to form an "ice castle."
5. Watch them throughout the day and see what happens.

Want to do more?

Place parts of the ice castle in different areas (i.e., in the sun, in the refrigerator, inside the room), and watch what occurs. Write an experience chart with the class on the activity. Freeze fruit juice into popsicles. Play Freeze Tag—children walk, run, hop or dance, then stop when "freeze" is called.

★ THE GIANT ENCYCLOPEDIA OF THEME ACTIVITIES

Snowjob

3+

Children explore the physical states of water. Understanding these processes is beyond young children, but exposure to them provides a basis for later comprehension. It also encourages close observation and real thinking. As a bonus, it can provide some entertaining conversation for the adults involved. Please don't laugh though; the children are serious.

Words to use

snow	ice
water	freeze
evaporate	melt
more	less

Materials

clear plastic glasses
snow
masking tape
markers

What to do

1. After a snowfall, ask the children to fill a plastic glass to the brim with snow. Bring it inside.
2. Ask the children what they think will happen to the snow. Expect a variety of answers. "It will turn into ice." "It will melt." "Nothing." "It will be water." Don't choose a correct answer; just encourage speculation.
3. As the snow begins to melt, ask the children what is happening. "It's turning to water," "It's getting little" and "It's going away" are typical answers. Look for observant remarks, but accept all comments.
4. Now ask why the snow is melting. If the children feel free to think and speculate, the answers can become really entertaining.

   "It must be the sun."
   "Well, let's pull down the shades then."
   "It's still melting."
   "Let's turn off the lights and close the door. Maybe that'll work."
   "Oh no! It's still getting to water!"

5. After much speculation and discussion, the adult may want to talk about temperature indoors and out, relating it to clothes worn, how hands feel or other familiar events.
6. Once the snow is melted, mark the much lower water level. The reason for the lower level can be demonstrated simply. Show the children a cupful of crumpled pieces of paper. Flatten the pieces out and show how much less space is used. They may not understand completely, but it does give them something to think over.
7. Next, ask the children what they think will happen when the water is put back outside. Some expect it to change back to snow, others will say ice. Do it and watch what happens. Again, don't explain; just observe.

★ HUG A TREE

The Big Melt Down   4+

Does salt melt snow and ice? Not really. The sun or warm weather does the melting. The salt lowers the temperature at which water freezes. In this activity children observe that salt has an effect on the freezing of water, and that is the reason it is used on sidewalks and streets during bad winter weather.

Words to use

salt   solution
temperature   freeze
melt   faster
color   blue
red

Materials

1 paper cup per child
food coloring (red and blue)
very cold water
salt
ice on the sidewalk or ground

What to do

1. Let children work in pairs. (Give each pair two cups so each child has one paper cup)
2. Ask them to prepare salt water solution in one cup—2 tablespoons of salt to 1 cup. Then fill with water and stir. Add one drop of red food coloring to designate that this cup contains the salt solution.
3. Now fill the second cup with water. Add one drop of blue food coloring.
4. Dress warmly, then go outside with one child carrying the salt (red) solution and the other carrying the plain (blue) water.
5. Now they pour the water in their cups onto the ice. We want to find out which one melts the most ice. Which one do you think will make the biggest hole? They can now return to the room and go back to check on this experiment later during the day.
6. Upon returning to their designated spot, they will observe that the salt solution has melted the ice. This is because salt water freezes at a lower temperature than ordinary water. In other words, it has to get colder than 32°F before salt water will freeze.

Want to do more?

Do the same activity using a thermometer.

Teaching tips

This activity is best on a sunny day after a snow or ice storm.

★ More Mudpies to Magnets

Thermometer Play

4+

Thermometers are one of the few scientific instruments children can learn to use independently. They begin by learning that the line gets longer when things are hot and shorter when things are cold. With minimal supervision and sturdy thermometers they can do quite a bit of experimenting on their own. They have plenty of time later to learn about all those numbers. In the meantime, let them explore!

Words to use

thermometer
hot
cold
warm
cool
rise
fall
degrees
Fahrenheit

Hot   warm   cool   cold

Materials

thermometer
4 similar containers
water
ice
towels
rubber bands
labeled pictures that show things that are cold, cool, warm and hot—they can show the four seasons
    or anything else you choose

What to do

1. Prepare four containers with the water temperatures suggested here. Be sure that the water is not hot enough to burn little hands. Place the labeled picture card behind each container.
   ✓ Hot (about 100°F)
   ✓ Warm (about 75°F)
   ✓ Cool (about 50°F)
   ✓ Cold (about 32°F) (you may need to float some ice in the water to achieve this temperature)
2. Place the thermometer in the cold container and wrap a rubber band around it where it registers the temperature.
3. Change the temperature by placing the thermometer into the hot water. Show the red line going up away from the rubber band.
4. Return the thermometer to the cooler container. It should return to its original position.
5. The conclusion is that the thermometer's marker changes as the temperature changes. The hotter the temperature the longer the red line on the thermometer.

6. Now it's time to experiment. Look at the picture behind the hot water bucket and at the word. Is the thermometer line going to be long or short? Hot or cold? Place the thermometer in the hot water watching what happens to the red line. The children could quickly test the water temperature with their finger. This is hot. Talk about the corresponding picture. Now go to the warm bucket and ask the same questions. The thermometer will drop and the temperature will be lower. Move through all the buckets matching and noting the respective temperature and pictures.

Want to do more?

Set up a temperature experiment station at the science table. Measure the temperature in different parts of the classroom. Start looking at the numbers. Chart the temperature daily. Bring in other kinds of thermometers and try them out.

★ MUDPIES TO MAGNETS

Grow a Rock   4+

Growing crystals is a way to teach children about the various forms of matter, how to make a solution and how to do a "real experiment" with the end result a treat—rock candy, pure sugar—but at least it has no artificial colorings or flavorings! The experiment can be done as a group activity, but it is more fun for the children if they can each grow their own candy rock. It's really not that much more work.

Words to use

crystal   solution
dissolve   saturated
solid   evaporate
experiment   stir
measure

Materials

sugar
cotton string
clear plastic cups or jars—8 ounce
    size works well
sticks or straws
water
spoons
masking tape
markers

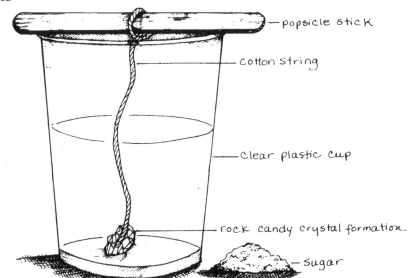

popsicle stick
cotton string
clear plastic cup
rock candy crystal formation
sugar

What to do

1. Fill the clear containers about two thirds full with very hot water.
    Note: Use extreme caution with hot water around children. We use hot water as it allows more sugar to dissolve.

Add sugar, a spoonful at a time, stirring until each spoonful is dissolved before adding the next. Keep adding sugar, a spoonful at a time, until no matter how much you stir, some sugar remains in the bottom of the cup. This is called a saturated solution. The water is saturated with sugar and will not hold any more. As you are making the solutions, ask the children where they think the sugar is going. What makes it disappear? Anybody have any ideas about how we could get it back? Explore the children's ideas. "You think the water makes the sugar disappear? How could we find out if it's really gone? Taste the cooking water. You're right! The sugar's just hiding; it dissolved."

2. Wet the string and tie a piece of it around a stick leaving enough hanging down to reach the bottom of the container (see illustration). Lay the stick across the top of the cup. Tell the children that we are going to get rid of the water so we can have our sugar back. What are their ideas on how this can or will happen? Write down some of their ideas, asking questions to help clarify their thoughts. Don't make any judgments. Instead, adopt a "let's watch and see what happens" attitude.

3. Place a piece of masking tape down the side of the cup and make a line to mark the water level. This will let the children note the change more easily. Tell the children that it will take many days for the water to go away. Mark the water level every other day or however often there is a noticeable change. It's obviously to your advantage to do this activity in dry weather! If you can place the cups near a radiator or other dry, cozy spot, so much the better. As you note changes, encourage the children's observations. Answers are not the goal. Most children don't really understand them anyway. Instead, stress "careful seeing," writing down descriptive comments. As the water starts to disappear, remind the children of other experiences they've had with evaporation such as clothes or paint drying, or puddles disappearing.

4. When the water is completely evaporated, compare the sugar crystals to table sugar. Break off some small pieces for the children to eat while you read some of the observations and ideas written about "growing sugar." The rest of the crystals can be sent home to share with family and friends.

Want to do more?

Cover one of the containers. How does that affect evaporation? Allow one to evaporate with no string. Experiment with other solutions—drink powders, salt, etc. Try the children's ideas. Not all substances produce crystals. Not all dissolve. Let them find that out for themselves.

★ MUDPIES TO MAGNETS

Cave in a Box   5+

Use winter's cold to create cave formations like those found underground. The ice grows one drop at a time to form stalactites and stalagmites. Patience and cold weather will reward you with your own cave to explore.

Words to use

freeze	temperature
cave	melt
stalactite	stalagmite
icicle	imagine
pretend	

Materials

eyedropper
food coloring
water
thick cotton string
small cardboard box

What to do

1. Build a cardboard box cave so that it can be attached to your window and retrieved on the coldest days of winter. Because you will be making your own icicles, your location must be a shady one, and since you will have to add water frequently, it should also be easily accessible.
2. Make a hole in the top of the box about 2 inches across. Tie the heavy cotton string to a stick, and hang the string through the opening until it is just above the bottom. This will serve as a wick and will make your icicle form much faster.
3. On one of your coldest days, begin to form an icicle by dripping water down the string a few drops at a time.
4. As the icicle builds up, talk with the children about how stalactites form from the ceiling of caves as the water, rich in minerals, drips down in one spot. As it flows and evaporates, it leaves its mineral deposits to form the features of the cave. If you have pictures of caves, share them with the children. They may have information of their own to add, too. As you continue to build the stalactite, add food coloring to the water. This simulates different mineral changes in the dripping water.
5. Just as your icicle forms over a long period of time, so the cave requires thousands, even millions of years to build. While the children may not relate to millions of years, they will see how long, doing it just a drop at a time, it takes to build their icicle.
6. Some of the water will drop to the bottom of the carton and a formation will appear. This is like a stalagmite.
7. If you have enough time and can cause the stalactite and stalagmite to meet, they form, in cave language, a column.

Want to do more?

Read a book on caves. Visit a cave. Make a classroom cave and talk about cave-dwelling animals. See slides or movies of a cave. Make up a story about your cave. Try a freezer for this activity.

★ MUDPIES TO MAGNETS

Snack and Cooking Activities

Sweet Honey   3+

Children learn about the taste of honey.

Words to use

honey
tastes
sticky
sweet
bread
spread
knife
honey comb
bees
hive

Materials

Sleepy Bear by Lydia Dabcovich
toaster
bread
honey
margarine
knives for spreading
honey jars

What to do

1. Ask the children what Sleepy Bear loved to eat. What brought him out of his cave in the spring?
2. Serve the toast, and if they want margarine, they can spread it.
3. Show the children a variety of honey jars: a plastic squeezable one that you snip the top off of to squeeze the honey out, a pottery jar with a wooden honey server that you twirl and honey in clear glass jars where you can see the honeycomb inside.
4. Ask the children to select one kind of honey. Let the children serve themselves.

Teaching tips

Discuss with the children that honey is a natural sweetener. The bees make it and store it in honeycombs, which we collect. Place the honey with the honeycomb in the jar on the science table for children to look at with their magnifying glasses.

★ STORY S-T-R-E-T-C-H-E-R-S

Making Soft Pretzels

3

Children learn how to measure and shape dough to make a delicious snack!

Words to use

pretzel   dough
twist   shape

Materials

large bowl
measuring cups and spoons
cookie sheet
aluminum foil
yeast
twisted pretzel (sample to show)
water
sugar
salt
flour
wax paper
beaten egg
kosher salt

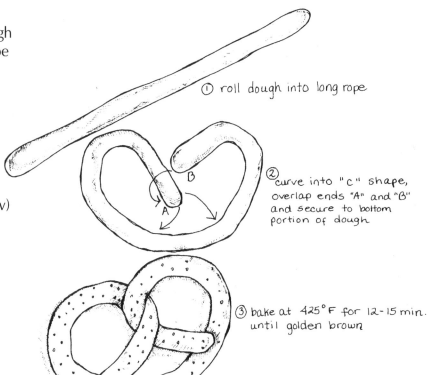

① roll dough into long rope

② curve into "c" shape, overlap ends "A" and "B" and secure to bottom portion of dough

③ bake at 425°F for 12-15 min. until golden brown

What to do

1. Line the cookie sheet with foil and preheat the oven to 425°F.
   Show the children a twisted pretzel. Discuss how the pretzel could be made.
2. Wash hands and prepare the pretzel dough.

> *1 packet yeast*
> *1 1/2 cups warm water*
> *1 tablespoon sugar*
> *1 teaspoon salt*
> *Stir in 4 cups flour.*
> *Knead the dough until smooth.*

3. Give each child a piece of wax paper for their workspace.
4. Pull off pieces of dough for each child to roll into a long rope that she can shape into a pretzel.
5. Place pretzels on a cookie sheet, coat with beaten egg and sprinkle with salt.
6. Bake at 425°F for 12-15 minutes until golden brown. Cool and serve.

Want to do more?

Art: Make pretzels from playdough.
Math: Categorize pretzels by sizes and shapes. Sequence the steps for making pretzels.
Sensory: Compare the taste of various pretzels—soft, hard, twists, sticks and nuggets.

★ THE GIANT ENCYCLOPEDIA OF CIRCLE TIME AND GROUP ACTIVITIES

JANUARY

snack & cooking activities

Making Peanut Butter

3+

Children learn measuring skills while making a delicious snack.

Words to use

measure
blend
salt
spread

Materials

peanuts
blender
measuring cups and spoons
cooking oil
salt
crackers
knife

What to do

1. Place one cup of peanuts in a blender or food processor.
2. Add a teaspoon of cooking oil.
3. Blend.
4. If you didn't use salted peanuts, you may want to add 1/4 teaspoon salt.
5. Spread on crackers, eat and enjoy!

★ WHERE IS THUMBKIN?

Popping Popcorn

3+

Children learn how popcorn changes when cooked, and they also get to taste it for snack.

Words to use

popcorn   hot
kernel   size
pop

Materials

cob of popcorn and cob of regular corn, if possible
popcorn popper
large bowl
popcorn kernels
paper cups

What to do

1. If possible, pass around a cob of popcorn and a cob of regular corn. Discuss the characteristics of each: size, texture, shape, smell.
2. Discuss what happens when popcorn is heated.
3. Pour popcorn into the popper and count how long it takes for the first kernel to pop. Discuss the smell of popcorn popping.
Note: Keep children away from the hot popcorn popper.
4. Fill paper cups with popcorn and give to the children.
5. Discuss what happened to the popcorn and how it tastes. Compare the characteristics of the popped corn to the unpopped kernels.

Want to do more?

Language: As the children describe the characteristics of the popcorn, write a list of descriptive words.
Math: Using a clock, time how long it takes the first kernel to pop.
Music: Play music and ask the children to dance to the music pretending they are kernels popping.
Science: Plant kernels of popcorn and chart the growth once the kernels sprout. Compare and contrast regular corn, Indian corn and popcorn.

★ THE GIANT ENCYCLOPEDIA OF CIRCLE TIME AND GROUP ACTIVITIES

Snowmen and Snowwoman Cookies   3+

Children learn to decorate sugar cookies

Words to use

dough
flatten
bake
decorate

Materials

ingredients for sugar cookie recipe or prepackaged rolls of cookies
rolling pin
round cookie or biscuit cutters
cookie sheet
wax paper
spatula
oven
variety of decorations: sprinkles, raisins, peanuts, licorice twists
Sadie and the Snowman by Allen Morgan

What to do

1. Roll out or flatten the cookie dough, leaving the dough a bit thick, and use different sized cookie or biscuit cutters to cut out the three balls for the snowman's and the snowwoman's bodies.
2. Bake the cookies following the recipe or package directions, being careful not to over-bake.
3. Tear one sheet of wax paper per child.
4. Remove the cookies from the oven; lift each one onto a separate sheet of wax paper to cool.
5. Place the decorations on the snack table and let the children decorate their snowmen or snow-women. Discuss how their cookies look like Sadie's.

Want to do more?

Create a large version of Sadie's snowman by using half of the cookie dough to create a snowman and the other half to make a snowwoman. Improvise large cookie cutters from mixing bowls. Let the children assist in decorating.

★ STORY S-T-R-E-T-C-H-E-R-S

Snowy Mashed Potatoes   3+

Children learn to mix instant mashed potatoes

Words to use

potatoes
mashed
snack

Materials

raw vegetables
knife and cutting board
package of instant mashed potatoes
liquid and dry measuring cups and spoons
mixing bowls

What to do

1. Encourage a small group of children to assist you in washing, peeling, slicing and arranging raw vegetables on a serving plate.
2. With a few children at a time, prepare single servings of instant mashed potatoes as directed on the package. Let each child mix his own mashed potatoes in an individual serving bowl.
3. Encourage the children who prepared their potatoes together to sit together at a snack table and eat raw vegetables with the potatoes.

Teaching tips

If one serving of mashed potatoes is too much per child, halve the recipe, or have two children work together preparing the potatoes and then divide their serving. If you think mashed potatoes are too unusual for snack, then serve ice cream to remind the children of snow.

★ STORY S-T-R-E-T-C-H-E-R-S

 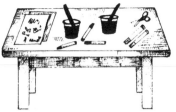

Transition Activities

The Snap Rap   3+

This snappy rap focuses children's attention. As children join in with the steady beat, they are encouraged to listen and follow directions.

Words to use

snap
fingers
chant

Materials

What to do

1. Simply start snapping your fingers.
2. When the children are looking and snapping along, say the following chant.

> *If you want to hear a story, (snap to the beat)*
> *This is what you do.*
> *You've got to sit down on the rug*
> *Like the children do.*
> *You've got to listen to your teacher,*
> *Raise your hand.*
> *You've got to let her know*
> *That you understand.*
> *That's right, (snap and point to children following directions)*
> *That's right.*
> *That's right.*
> *That's right.*

Want to do more?

For children who can't snap, simply clap to the beat. Change the words to what the children are expected to do. For example, "If you want to go outside, this is what you do. You've got to line up at the door like the soldiers do." Do the Magic Clap. Tell the children that whenever you clap a pattern, they should stop, repeat it and look at you. Practice a few times, then give it a try on the playground or in the classroom when you need their attention.

★ TRANSITION TIME

Little Mouse

3+

Pull this little mouse out of a pocket to quiet children for stories or other activities. Children will lower their voices so they don't scare the little mouse.

Words to use

mouse
little
quiet

Materials

old cloth glove
felt scraps
markers or paint pens
scissors
glue

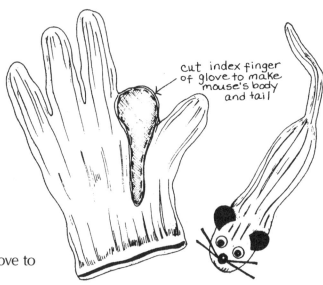

cut index finger of glove to make mouse's body and tail

What to do?

1. In advance, cut off the index finger of the glove to make the mouse's body and tail.
2. Cut out ears from felt and glue them on.
3. Draw on eyes, a nose and whiskers.
4. Stick an index finger in the mouse puppet, then hide it behind your back.
5. In a soft voice, begin the fingerplay and slowly creep the mouse out from behind you.

> *A little mouse (hold up right index finger and wiggle)*
> *Lived quietly in his hole.*
> *A little mouse (make a hole with left hand and stick the right finger in it)*
> *Lived quietly in his hole.*
> *When all was as quiet,*
> *As quiet as could be—*
> *Sh! Sh! Sh!*
> *Out popped he! (pull out right finger and wiggle)*

Want to do more?

Make a bunny puppet or a caterpillar puppet from the other fingers of the glove.

★ TRANSITION TIME

Teeny Tiny Friends   3+

Teeny Tiny Friends is another technique that helps focus children's attention.
These imaginary characters give children a reason to talk softly.

Words to use

teeny
tiny
friend
listen
quiet

Materials

old pocketbook, bag or box
small toy figures (dolls, animals or anything that would interest the children)

What to do

1. Place the toys in the bag or box.
2. Before the story, tell the children you have brought some little friends to visit with them, but the friends are very tiny and have teeny ears, so they will have to use tiny voices.
3. When the children are quiet, carefully remove the toy figures from the box or pocket book.
4. If the children start to become too loud say, "Remember our little friends. Let's not hurt their little ears."
5. When the story is over, have the children say good-bye to the tiny friends and return them to the bag or box.

Want to do more?

Tiny friends might come out at nap time and rest with children, or they might visit other activities in your room. Have children make up names for the friends and tell imaginary stories about them.

★ TRANSITION TIME

I'll Find a Friend   3+

Start the day with this song or use it to change activities. The activity encourages
children to feel part of the group and develop social skills.

Words to use

friend
school
move

What to do

1. Ask each child to find a friend to help him do the movements to the song.
2. Sing the following to the tune of "Farmer in the Dell."

> *I'll find a friend at school. (two or three children get together and hold*
> *hands)*
> *I'll find a friend at school.*
> *I'm so glad I came today.*
> *I'll find a friend at school.*
>
> *We'll skip around the room.... (children hold hands and skip)*
> *We'll jump up and down.... (children jump together)*
> *We'll tiptoe around the room.... (children tiptoe)*

3. Continue singing, adding other motions.
4. End with this verse.

> *We'll sit down quietly. (sit down on rug)*
> *We'll sit down quietly.*
> *I'm so glad I have a friend.*
> *We'll sit down quietly.*

Want to do more?

Help shy children or other children who have difficulty finding a friend to play with to find a partner. Change the words of the last verse to direct the children to other activities such as "It's time to go outside" or "We'll wash our hands for lunch."

★ TRANSITION TIME

Puppet Pals and Inspectors   3+

Check to see if everything is in its place with a puppet pal or inspector. Children enjoy taking responsibility for making sure the room is cleaned properly. In addition, giving children responsibility empowers them and makes the classroom less authoritarian.

Words to use

pal
inspect
clean up

Materials

hand puppet or stuffed animal

What to do

1. When children are just about through cleaning up, put the puppet on your hand and let the puppet go around the room and inspect various centers.
2. Talk in the voice of the puppet, or let the puppet pretend to whisper in your ear and repeat what it says to the class.
3. Give positive comments such as, "Puppet Pal likes the way all the puzzles have been put together," or a reminder like, "Puppet Pal sees some blocks we need to put on the shelf."
4. After modeling what to do with the puppet, let the children take turns using it to inspect the room and give feedback to the other children.

Want to do more?

Make a badge for the inspector. Give the child a note pad to "write down" what needs to be done. Assign a child to be "playground inspector." The inspector goes around and checks to see if all the toys have been put away after play.

★ TRANSITION TIME

Listen to the Snow   3+

Develops children's' coordination.

Words to use

fingers
lip
eyes
snow
quiet
fall
blink
flutter

Materials

What to do

Help children quiet down with this wonderful fingerplay.

> *Shhh, be quiet and listen to the snow. (put your index finger to your lip)*
> *It's softly falling down, you know. (wiggle your fingers like falling snow)*
> *Shhh, be quiet and blink your eyes (blink your eyes)*
> *While white flakes flutter from the skies. (wiggle your fingers like falling snow)*

★ 500 FIVE MINUTE GAMES

Oh, Doctor Jane

3+

This activity develops children's imagination.

Words to use

doctor
dialogue

Materials

What to do

1. Divide the children into two groups.
2. Let them suggest how to act out the dialogue.

> *Group One: Oh, Doctor Jane.*
> *Group Two: Oh, Doctor Jane.*

3. Continue with Group One speaking a line and Group Two repeating it.

> *I've got pain. (repeat)*
> *My head is hot. (repeat)*
> *I don't want a shot. (repeat)*
> *Oh, Doctor Jane. (repeat)*
> *I've got pain. (repeat)*
> *Please help me, Doctor, to get better. (both groups together)*
> *Open up wide. (repeat)*
> *Let's look inside. (repeat)*
> *Your throat is red. (repeat)*
> *Better go to bed. (repeat)*
> *And drink your milk. (repeat)*
> *And get some rest. (repeat)*
> *You will feel better in the morning. (both groups together)*
> *By Jackie Silberg*

★ 500 FIVE MINUTE GAMES

Hot Potato

3+

Play this "hot" game just for fun. Children learn to listen and develop motor skills as they play Hot Potato.

Words to use

pass　　　　　　hot
music　　　　　stop

Materials

beanbag
music (tape or record)

What to do

1. Have the children sit in a circle and begin passing the beanbag around as the music is played.
2. Stop the music.
3. Whoever is holding the beanbag is out of the game. (That child can just scoot back from the circle or can be dismissed to another activity.) Or play a noncompetitive version by asking children to name rhyming words, favorite foods, pets or other categories if they are caught holding the beanbag when the music stops.
4. The game continues until there is one child left.

★ TRANSITION TIME

Four Corners

3+

*Give children the opportunity to get up and move around with Four Corners.
This is a game of luck that everyone will want to play.*

Words to use

corner
freeze
tiptoe

Materials

What to do

1. Number each of the corners in the room: 1, 2, 3 and 4.
2. Choose one person to be "it."
3. He hides his eyes.
4. As "it" counts slowly from one to ten, everyone else tiptoes to a corner in the room.
5. When "it" says "freeze" (after counting to ten), everyone must be in a corner.
6. "It" then calls out the number of a corner (1, 2, 3 or 4) and the children in that corner are out of the game and must sit down in the "stew pot" in the middle of the room.
7. "It" begins counting to ten again as everyone moves to a new corner.
8. The game continues until there is one person left, and that person then become the new "it."

★ TRANSITION TIME

Follow My Tracks

3+

This activity increases children's balance and coordination.

Words to use

footprints
step
follow

Materials

an untracked area of snow

What to do

1. Have one child walk around on the playground in a random way.
2. Encourage the child to take small and large steps and to move in different directions.
3. You might provide an example first.
4. Then challenge another child to follow exactly in the first child's footprints.

★ THE OUTSIDE PLAY AND LEARNING BOOK

Footprints in the Snow

3+

The children will see positive and negative designs looking at the boot sole itself and the print it makes on the ground. It takes balance and coordination to walk in someone else's footprints. The children may also become more conscious of shapes and designs.

Words to use

footprint	track
step	big
boot	small

Materials

fresh snow

What to do

1. Let the children notice how their boots make tracks in the snow.
2. Let one child at a time walk in the snow and notice how the boot prints differ.
3. How much bigger are the teacher's tracks?
4. Later on, can the children guess whose boots made which tracks?

Want to do more?

Invite the children to search the playground and see if there are any animal tracks or bird tracks to notice. Make some decorative patterns in the snow with footprints. If you have tires on your playground, roll them, and let the children look at the pattern of the tire tracks. See if the children can follow exactly in someone else's boot tracks.

★ THE OUTSIDE PLAY AND LEARNING BOOK

Hide the Mitten   3+

Children learn matching skills, an important math skill, in this activity.

Words to use

mittens
match
hide
find

Materials

one bright-colored pair of mittens
The Three Little Kittens retold by Paul Galdone

What to do

1. Let the children know the previous day that when they come in the next day, one of the mittens will be hidden somewhere in the classroom.
2. Have your assistant hide one mitten from the pair each morning while the children are listening to you reading *The Three Little Kittens.*
3. Lay the unhidden mitten out in plain sight as a reminder to hunt for the other one.

★ THEMESTORMING

Mitten Safari   3+

Children learn observation skills while playing this game.

Words to use

pair
match

Materials

real mittens or mitten pairs cut from wallpaper sample books, one per child

What to do

1. Hide one mitten of each pair in the classroom.
2. Distribute the leftover mittens to the children and instruct them to find the lost mitten.
3. Remind the children not to pick up a mitten that does not match theirs.

★ THEMESTORMING

Sleigh Ride

4

Children learn how to gallop.

Words to use

gallop
skip
practice
horse
sleigh
snow

Material

music such as "Sleigh Ride" by Leroy Anderson or "Troika" from the "Lieutenant Kije Suite" by
   Prokofiev

What to do

1. This musical game is a little easier for four and five year olds than for younger children.
2. Because galloping usually precedes skipping, this game offers good practice for skipping.
3. Composer Leroy Anderson wrote a wonderful piece of music called "Sleigh Ride." Play the music
   for the children and tell them it is about horses pulling a sleigh through the snow.
4. Let the children move to the music however they please.
5. Then show them how to gallop by placing one foot in front of the other and moving to the music.
6. Another wonderful piece of music for this activity is the "Troika" from the "Lieutenant Kije Suite"
   by Prokofiev.

Hide and Seek Tracking

4+

This is great fun for children and may be surprisingly difficult at first. There is a certain amount of logic required for this game. The children need to see the relationship of cause and effect (tracks are made when you walk) and to follow a path to its conclusion.

Materials

a "treasure" to hide (a plate of cookies maybe)
an untracked playground after a fresh snow

What to do

1. When the snow is fresh, before the children go outside, go out to the playground and hide a "treasure" somewhere.
2. Walk around and about to make your tracks go in interesting patterns and different directions before you finally hide the treasure.
3. Then carefully retrace your steps back to the door.
4. Let the children out and see if they can follow your tracks to find the treasure.
5. Can they figure this out by themselves?

Want to do more?

When the children are thoroughly familiar with this game, let one of the children be the person to hide the treasure. This could also be a fun version of "hide and seek." Let three or four children out a minute before the others, and have them hide somewhere. Then let the other children follow their tracks to find them.

★ THE OUTSIDE PLAY AND LEARNING BOOK

Still Water

4+

This activity works best with small groups. With a group of more than nine, do the actiivty until about half the children have been blindfolded. The others can have a turn the next day.

Words to use

names
gentle
group
class
blindfold
volunteer

Materials

blindfold

What to do

1. Form a small circle of five to nine children. Explain the rules for the activity. Blindfold a volunteer who stands in the center of the circle. The rest of the children hold hands and begin walking in a circle while softly chanting, "Around, around, around we go, and where we stop (name of blindfolded child) won't know!"

2. After a few moments, the child in the center of the circle says, "Still water!" The circle then stops moving. The blindfolded child walks forward until she touches someone in the circle. After exploring the other child's head and clothes, the blindfolded child tries to guess that child's name.

3. That child may choose to go into the center of the circle to begin the game again. Otherwise, call for volunteers until everyone has had a turn being blindfolded.

4. Emphasize the idea of gentleness when the blindfolded child touches another. Younger children may be unintentionally rough. Watch carefully and guide the child if necessary.

5. If the blindfolded child has difficulty identifying the child in the circle, ask the child to say a few words to provide a clue.

Want to do more?

To make the activity more difficult, ask the children to extend their hands gently toward the blindfolded person. See if she can guess a child's name just by touching hands. Or reverse roles by asking all those in the circle to close their eyes. Choose someone to go into the center. This child can open her eyes. Ask those in the circle to join hands and walk slowly around. Now when the circle stops at "Still water," the child in the center will touch a child in the circle, who will have to guess her name.

★ THE PEACEFUL CLASSROOM

My Friend   4+

This game encourages a sense of belonging and reinforces the learning of each other's names. If there is an odd number of children, join the activity to create two groups of equal size. You will need at least fourteen children for this activity.

Words to use

names   gentle
group   equal
class   inner
outer   join

Materials

music

What to do

1. Divide the children into two groups of equal size. One group joins hands and stretches to make their circle as wide as possible. The second group goes to the center and forms a second circle, facing the first.

2. When the music starts, the children in the outer circle begin to rotate in one direction while the children in the center close their eyes. When the music stops, the children in the outer circle stop and drop their hands. The children in the inner circle open their eyes, drop their hands and run to stand in front of the person facing them in the outer circle. Each child should have only one partner.

3. As soon as partners are determined, ask each child from the inner circle to name the child facing him, quickly, one after the other.

4. When the music starts again, children who were in the outer circle go to the center, while those who were in the center turn to face inward, join hands and begin circling around the others.

Want to do more?

Try switching the roles of the two circles. The inner and outer circles can both face the center and rotate in opposite directions. When the music stops, the children in the outer circle can stand behind those in the inner circle. The children in the inner circle would not immediately know who was going to name them.

Book to read

No Friends by James Stevenson

Home connection

Parents can involve their children in a family guessing game. A parent can begin by thinking of someone in the family and giving the child a clue, for example, "I am thinking about someone who really loves spaghetti." Keep giving clues until the child guesses correctly.

★ THE PEACEFUL CLASSROOM

Cookie Machine   4+

Young children need a history of cooperation to prepare them to cope with the pressures of competition.

Words to use

cooperate
volunteer
join
help
imagine
cookie
chef
ingredients
bake

Materials

small, sturdy area rug

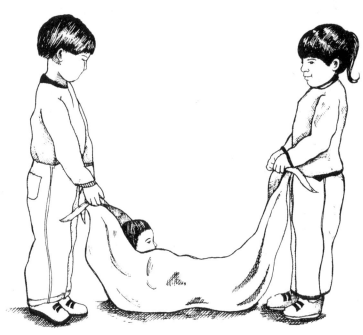

games

What to do

1. Invite the children to cooperate to make an imaginary "cookie machine." Ask for one volunteer to be the "cookie" and two volunteers to be "chefs."
2. Ask the remaining children to sit in two equal lines about three feet apart. They represent the ingredients. Place the rug at one end between the lines. Ask the "cookie" what kind of cookie—oatmeal, raisin, chocolate chip—she would like to be. Ask the "cookie" to lie on her back on the rug.
3. When the "cookie" and the "chefs" are ready, and each part of the machine knows what ingredient they are to contribute, then begin. For example, some children will put in the flour, some the sugar, others the raisins and chocolate chips. The final four children can be the oven, joining hands over the cookie and humming as it "bakes."
4. Ask the "chefs" to pull the rug holding the cookie between the lines to the other end, where it will be baked. Offer help if needed.
5. Repeat with another volunteer. If you have enough children, you can have two cookies on the production line, one after the other.

★ THE PEACEFUL CLASSROOM

Cooperative Towers   4+

Our educational system is based on competition. Children are often pitted against each other in competing to be the first with the "right" answer. One child's failure to answer "correctly" becomes another's opportunity to succeed. This activity teaches children a healthy alternative—cooperation and negotiation.

Words to use

cooperate
partner
balance
tower

Materials

several small wooden blocks, cut in various irregular sizes

What to do

1. Invite the children to try a difficult cooperative game. Demonstrate by asking one child to be your partner. Begin by placing one block in the center of the table. Ask your partner to choose a block and place it on top of the one you just played.
2. If she succeeds, the turn passes back to you. You have to place a third block on the tower, either upon the first or second block.
3. Turns pass back and forth with each person attempting to balance an additional block on the tower.
4. Players can place blocks anywhere on the tower that they wish, as long as the first block played is the only block to touch the table. Once the tower collapses, the game is over. Count the number of blocks balanced and suggest trying to improve the score the next time.

Want to do more?

Limit the number of blocks to about twenty. Be sure to include several dowel rods of various widths and lengths to increase the challenge. You can increase the number of children in a group from two to four or five. This activity can be made easier by increasing the size of the blocks and cutting them to a uniform shape. The more slender the dowel rod, the more difficult the task.

Book to read

The Quarreling Book by Charlotte Zolotow

★ THE PEACEFUL CLASSROOM

Crossing the Bridge   4+

This activity teaches children how to work together to solve a problem.

Words to use

cooperate
problem
solve
help
group

Materials

two 8′ lengths of 1″ x 6″ boards—each board should be equal in length to a line of half your children standing side by side

What to do

1. Tell the children that you have a difficult problem for them to solve. Lay the boards flat, end to end, in a straight line. Ask half the group to line up on each board. Once everyone is on board, say, "Let's pretend you are a bridge. Let's see if everyone on one part of the bridge can get to the other side of the bridge. Help each other as much as you can. Do not step off the bridge until everyone has changed sides."
2. In the second round, lay the boards parallel to each other and about two feet apart. Challenge the children to cross from one bridge to the other.

Want to do more?

With older children, raise each bridge about three inches off the ground using building blocks. This increases the drama of the activity. Increase the width of the boards to make the activity easier.

Book to read

Burgoo Stew by Susan Patron

★ THE PEACEFUL CLASSROOM

Night Train   5+

Night Train combines three different but complementary skills. The engine has to protect the cars as it moves through the forest, while the trees provide warnings. The engine and cars have to cooperate to remain intact as the whole train moves. The train is delivering the toys to help children in the town.

Words to use

help
protect
cooperation
teamwork

Materials

extra belts or ropes cut to serve as belts
three hats
three blindfolds
The Little Engine That Could by Watty Piper

What to do

1. If possible, to introduce the activity, read *The Little Engine That Could* by Watty Piper, illustrated by George and Doris Hauman (Platt and Munk, 1954).
2. Tell the children that they are going to pretend to be a train bringing toys for children who live in a town on the other side of a forest. But this train is moving at night, and only the engine has a light to see.
3. Ask for a volunteer to be the engine and three others to be the train cars. The remaining children are trees in the forest. Leave enough room between the trees to ensure safety. Tell the trees that they are not to move. They can make an "ooooo" sound if any train car is about to bump into them. Place hats on three of the trees. Tell the engine they must go around the trees with hats before they can leave the forest.
4. The cars line up behind the engine and hold onto the belt of the person in front of them. Provide belts or a loop of rope if necessary. When the train is ready, blindfold each of the cars. Emphasize that the engine should move slowly. Supervise closely.
5. Stand on the other side of the forest and tell the train you are the town they have to reach. Ask them to begin.
6. Let the children take turns being the engine.

Want to do more?

To increase the challenge, operate two trains at the same time (if you have enough children), add more cars to the engine and/or bring the trees closer together. Increasing the difficulty requires closer supervision. You may also conduct the activity without blindfolds in a darkened room or outside at night. Give the engine a flashlight.

★ THE PEACEFUL CLASSROOM

Fox and Geese Game   5+

This is a game of tag that will be especially enjoyed by older children. Children learn that it takes longer to run around a circle than to run across it. (The shortest distance between two points is a straight line!) This game also requires good balance.

Words to use

circle
tracks
quarters
center
run
tag
safe

Materials

an untracked area of snow

What to do

1. On an untracked snow area, walk in a large circle to make a circle track.
2. Then intersect the circle, to cut it into quarters.
3. The center of the circle is the safe place.
4. The children may run only on the tracks.
5. It tries to tag another player, but if the player reaches the center before she is tagged, she is safe.
6. If a player is tagged, she becomes It.

★ THE OUTSIDE PLAY AND LEARNING BOOK

Books

Animals of the Night by Merry Banks
Bread and Jam for Frances by Russell Hoban
Caps, Hats, Socks, and Mittens by Louise Borden
Chicken Soup with Rice by Maurice Sendak
The First Snowfall by Anne and Harlow Rockwell
Fox Went Out on a Chilly Night by Peter Spier
Fox's Dream by Keizaburo Tejima
The Giant Jam Sandwich by John V. Lord and Janet Burroway
Hand Rhymes by Marc Brown
Here Are My Hands by Bill Martin Jr. and John Archambault
Keep Looking by Millicent Selsam and Joyce Hunt
The Mitten by Alvin Tresselt
Ollie's Ski Trip by Elsa Beskow
One Fine Day by Nonny Hogrogian
Peanut Butter and Jelly by Nadine Wescott Bernard
Sadie and the Snowman by Allen Morgan
The Snowy Day by Ezra Jack Keats
Something Is Going To Happen by Charlotte Zolotow
Stopping by Woods on a Snowy Evening by Robert Frost
The Three Little Kittens by Lorinda Cauley Bryan
Three Little Kittens by Paul Galdone
Thumbelina by Hans Christian Anderson
The Tomten by Astrid Lindgren
White Snow, Bright Snow by Alvin Tresselt
Winter Magic by Eveline Hasler

Records, Tapes and CDs

Beall, Pamela Conn and Susan Hagen Nipp. "Fox Went Out on a Chilly Night" from *Wee Sing Silly Songs*. Price Stern Sloan, 1986.

Beall, Pamela Conn and Susan Hagen Nipp. "Where Is Thumbkin?" from *Wee Sing Children's Songs and Fingerplays*. Price Stern Sloan, 1979.

Beall, Pamela Conn and Susan Hagen Nipp. "Three Little Kittens" from *Wee Sing Nursery Rhymes and Lullabies*. Price Stern Sloan, 1985.

Jenkins, Ella. "No More Pie" from *Play Your Instruments and Make a Pretty Sound*. Folkways, 1968.

Scruggs, Joe. "Peanut Butter" from *Late Last Night*. Educational Graphics Press, 1984.

Sharon, Lois and Bram. "Where Is Thumbkin?" from *One, Two, Three, Four, Live!* Elephant, 1982.

Weissman, Jackie. "Peanut Butter" from *Miss Jackie and Her Friends Sing about Peanut Butter, Tarzan and Roosters*. Miss Jackie, 1981.

"Count My Fingers" from *Songs About Me*. Kimbo.

FEBRUARY

 # Fingerplays, Poems and Songs

Hey, Diddle, Diddle

Hey, diddle, diddle, the cat and the fiddle,
The cow jumped over the moon;
The little dog laughed to see such sport,
And the dish ran away with the spoon.

★ ONE POTATO, TWO POTATO, THREE POTATO, FOUR

Wee Willie Winkie

Wee Willie Winkie runs through the town,
Upstairs and downstairs in his nightgown.
Rapping at the window, crying through the lock,
"Are the children in their beds?
For it's past eight o'clock!"

★ ONE POTATO, TWO POTATO, THREE POTATO, FOUR

Deedle, Deedle, Dumpling

Deedle, deedle, dumpling, my son John
Went to bed with his breeches on.
One shoe off and one shoe on;
Deedle, deedle, dumpling, my son John.

★ ONE POTATO, TWO POTATO, THREE POTATO, FOUR

Engine, Engine, Number Nine

Engine, engine, number nine,
Ring the bell when it's time.
O-U-T spells out goes he
Into the middle of the dark blue sea.

Engine, engine, number nine,
Running on Chicago line.
When she's polished, she will shine.
Engine, engine, number nine.

Engine, engine, number nine,
Running on Chicago line.
If the train should jump the track,
Do you want your money back?

Engine, engine, number nine,
Running on Chicago line.
See it sparkle, see it shine,
Engine, engine, number nine.

If the train should jump the track,
Will I get my money back?
Yes, no, maybe so.

★ ONE POTATO, TWO POTATO, THREE POTATO, FOUR

Five Red Valentines

Five red valentines from the ten cent store.
I sent one to mother, and now there are four.
Four red valentines, pretty ones to see.
I gave one to brother, so now there are three.
Three red valentines that say I love you.
I gave one to sister, and now there are two.
Two red valentines, my, we have fun.
I gave one to daddy, and now there is one.
One red valentine and the story is almost done.
I gave it to baby, and now there is none.

★ TRANSITION TIME

The Wheels on the Bus (The Bus Song)

The people on the bus go up and down,
Up and down, up and down.
The people on the bus go up and down,
All around the town.

The wiper on the bus goes, "Swish, swish, swish,
Swish, swish, swish, swish, swish, swish"....

The brake on the bus goes, "Roomp, roomp,
    roomp,
Roomp, roomp, roomp, roomp, roomp, roomp"....

The money on the bus goes, "Clink, clink, clink,
Clink, clink, clink, clink, clink, clink"....

The wheels on the bus go round and round,
Round and round, round and round....

The baby on the bus goes, "Wah, wah, wah,
Wah, wah, wah, wah, wah, wah"....

★ WHERE IS THUMBKIN?

Down by the Station

Down by the station
Early in the morning,
See the little puffer bellies
All in a row.

See the engine driver
Pull the little throttle,
Puff, puff. Toot! Toot!
Off we go.

★ WHERE IS THUMBKIN?

Color Song

Tune: "I've Been Working on the Railroad"

Red is the color for an apple to eat.
Red is the color for cherries, too.
Red is the color for strawberries,
I like red, don't you?

Blue is the color for the big blue sky.
Blue is the color for baby things, too.
Blue is the color of my sister's eyes,
I like blue, don't you?

Yellow is the color for the great big sun.
Yellow is the color for lemonade, too.
Yellow is the color of a baby chick,
I like yellow, don't you?

Green is the color for the leaves on the trees.
Green is the color for green peas, too.
Green is the color of a watermelon,
I like green, don't you?

Orange is the color for oranges.
Orange is the color for carrots, too.
Orange is the color for a jack-o-lantern,
I like orange, don't you?

Purple is the color for a bunch of grapes.
Purple is the color for grape juice, too.
Purple is the color for a violet,
I like purple, don't you?

★ WHERE IS THUMBKIN?

Are You Sleeping?

Are you sleeping,
Are you sleeping,
Brother John, Brother John?
Morning bells are ringing,
Morning bells are ringing,
Ding, ding, dong!
Ding, ding, dong!

★ WHERE IS THUMBKIN?

Twinkle, Twinkle, Little Star

Twinkle, twinkle, little star,
How I wonder what you are,
Up above the world so high,
Like a diamond in the sky.
Twinkle, twinkle, little star,
How I wonder what you are.

★ WHERE IS THUMBKIN?

February Learning Centers

Grocery Store Center

While playing in the Grocery Store Center children learn:

1. About the world in which they live.
2. To use real experiences in their play.
3. To expand their language as they use new vocabulary that relates to the grocery store.
4. About the operations of a grocery store and the work of the employees.

Suggested props for the Grocery Store Center

cash register
empty food containers such as
   canned food
   boxes of pasta
   milk carton
   jugs
   frozen food containers
   plastic jars
(Be sure to include food
   items that are frequently
   eaten by children in the
   classroom.)
plastic baskets
plastic fruit and vegetables
signs and displays from a
   grocery store
paper bags and plastic bags

Curriculum Connections

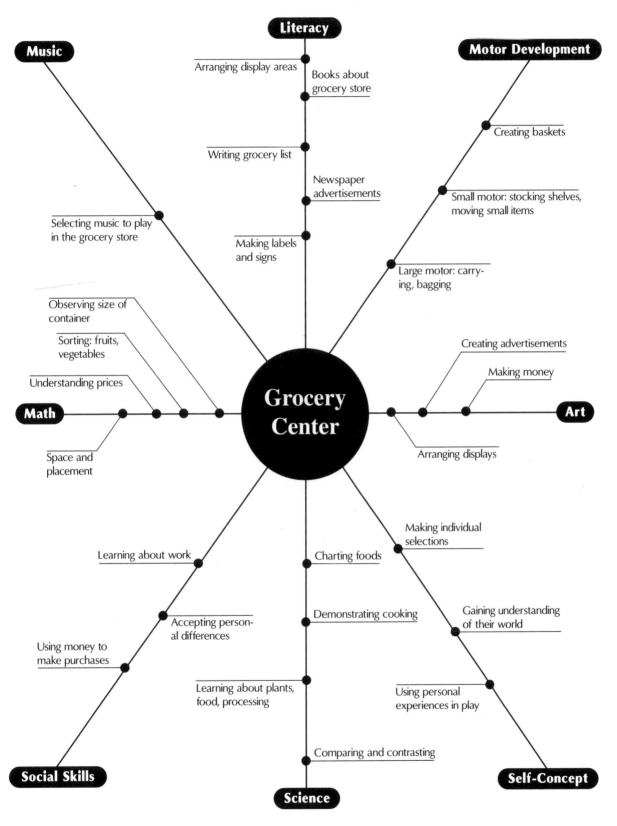

Music

Selecting music to play in the grocery store

Literacy

Arranging display areas

Books about grocery store

Writing grocery list

Newspaper advertisements

Making labels and signs

Motor Development

Creating baskets

Small motor: stocking shelves, moving small items

Large motor: carrying, bagging

Math

Observing size of container

Sorting: fruits, vegetables

Understanding prices

Space and placement

Grocery Center

Art

Creating advertisements

Making money

Arranging displays

Making individual selections

Charting foods

Demonstrating cooking

Gaining understanding of their world

Using personal experiences in play

Learning about work

Accepting personal differences

Using money to make purchases

Learning about plants, food, processing

Comparing and contrasting

Social Skills

Science

Self-Concept

★ THE COMPLETE LEARNING CENTER BOOK

Nighttime Center

While playing in the Nighttime Center children learn:

1. To enjoy quality children's books related to nighttime.
2. To experience pleasant activities related to nighttime.
3. To play out some of their experiences and fears.
4. That other children have positive and negative feelings about nighttime.

Suggested props for the Nighttime Center

roll of black shade cloth (inexpensive fabric used to keep grass from growing under walks or to
    provide shade for plants; can be bought at garden or home improvement stores)
small flashlights
air mattresses
glow-in-the-dark stickers such as moon and stars
stuffed toys and baby blankets
cassette player and recordings of soft, relaxing music
lamp
pillows, beanbag chair or lawn chair pads
large appliance box with many holes cut in the shape of stars to let in light
sheet, rope and clamp-on light to make a
    shadow stage
fuzzy fabric and fabric glue
rocking chair

Curriculum Connections

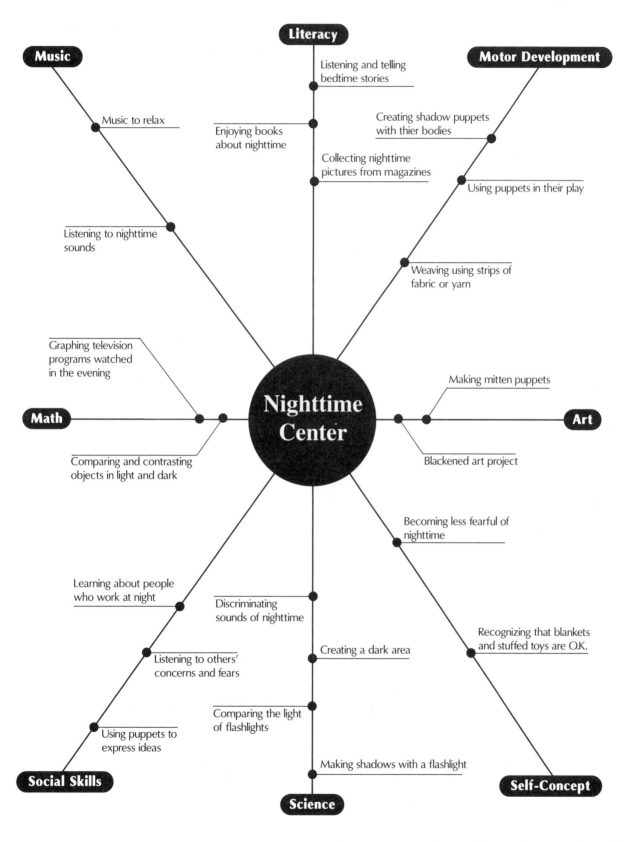

Music
- Music to relax
- Listening to nighttime sounds

Literacy
- Listening and telling bedtime stories
- Enjoying books about nighttime
- Collecting nighttime pictures from magazines

Motor Development
- Creating shadow puppets with thier bodies
- Using puppets in their play
- Weaving using strips of fabric or yarn

Math
- Graphing television programs watched in the evening
- Comparing and contrasting objects in light and dark

Nighttime Center

Art
- Making mitten puppets
- Blackened art project

Self-Concept
- Becoming less fearful of nighttime
- Recognizing that blankets and stuffed toys are O.K.

Social Skills
- Learning about people who work at night
- Listening to others' concerns and fears
- Using puppets to express ideas

Science
- Discriminating sounds of nighttime
- Creating a dark area
- Comparing the light of flashlights
- Making shadows with a flashlight

FEBRUARY

learning centers

Art Activities

Star Designs   3+

Children practice fine motor skills as they learn about star shapes.

Words to use

star	shape
templates	cut
trace	cardboard

Materials

drawing paper
crayons
star templates cut from cardboard

What to do

1. Provide the children with the star shapes cut from cardboard.
2. Encourage the children to use the star shapes as templates. As they trace around them, have them move the shapes around and even trace on top of already traced stars.
3. Changing colors of crayons used will add an interesting dimension.

★ WHERE IS THUMBKIN?

Torn Paper Silhouettes   3+

Children use their imaginations to create a light and dark picture.

Words to use

shape	tear
light	paste
dark	imagine

Materials

construction paper
paste or glue sticks
crayons

What to do

1. Provide each child with a large shape that has been randomly torn from light colored paper.
2. Children paste the shape on darker background art paper.
3. With crayons and imagination, children turn the shape into a picture. Younger children may just make a pretty design.

★ THE INSTANT CURRICULUM

Shoe Box Train   3+

Children learn to build their own train from shoe boxes.

Words to use

box
train
print
cut
window
wheel
round
square
transportation

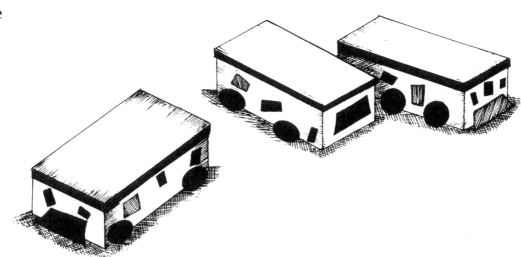

Materials

shoe boxes
tempera paints
paintbrushes
construction paper
scissors
glue

What to do

1. Ask the children to bring shoe boxes from home. Be sure to have extras for those children who forget to bring a box.
2. The children paint their shoe boxes.
3. When the boxes are dry, the children cut out construction paper windows and wheels.
4. Glue the windows and wheels to the shoe box train.

★ WHERE IS THUMBKIN?

art activities

Spool Painting

3+

Children learn about transportation-related shapes in this artistic activity.

Words to use

spool
bus shape
print

Materials

spools (those with spokes on the tops are best)
tempera paint
yellow construction paper cut into simple bus shapes

What to do

Encourage the children to use the spools to print wheels all over the bus-shaped paper.

★ WHERE IS THUMBKIN?

Tire Prints

3+

Children develop fine motor skills using spools to print on paper.

Words to use

spools
sponge
print

Materials

white paper
tempera paint (black)
empty spools
sponges

What to do

1. Pour mixed paint onto sponges and let it soak in.
2. Children choose one spool at a time and lightly press the spool onto sponge.
3. Press the spool onto paper to make tire prints.

Books to read

Boat Book by Gail Gibbons
The Little Red Engine That Could by Watty Piper
Teddy Bears Take the Train by Susanna Gretz and Alison Sage
The Biggest Truck by David Lyon

Constructing a Car

Children use their imaginations while constructing a car from various art supplies.

Words to use

box	car
model	build
make	construct
window	door
wheel	vehicle
road	transportation

Materials

small box, one per child
paints of various colors
paintbrushes
glue
markers
assortment of small construction paper shapes

What to do

1. Have the children bring small boxes from home.
2. Cut out small construction paper shapes that are proportional to the size of the boxes.
3. Talk to children about how people usually move from one place to another. Show a finished car model and discuss how you made it.
4. Have children paint the boxes and let them dry.
5. Have the children glue on shapes for wheels, doors and windows.
6. After the glue dries, use markers to draw in other features.

Want to do more?

Use large butcher paper and markers to create a town. Children can help draw roads, buildings, etc. Use constructed vehicles to move around the neighborhood. Let children display finished products and tell others in the group about their vehicles.

Books to read

Away We Go illustrated by Irene Friedman
The Great Big Car and Truck Book illustrated by Richard Scarry

Song to sing

"Wheels on the Bus"

★ THE GIANT ENCYCLOPEDIA OF THEME ACTIVITIES

FEBRUARY

art activities

Tissue Contact

3+

Children practice fine motor skills while making these lovely designs.

Words to use

sticky	collage
rectangle	trim
design	shapes
heart	punch
hole	yarn
hang	Valentine

Materials

clear contact paper
art tissue, variety of colors
scissors
hole punch
yarn
collage items such as bits of lace, thread, confetti, glitter or hole punches, optional

What to do

1. Cut a rectangle of clear contact paper about 6 x 12 inches, or any other size.
2. Fold the rectangle in half. Peel the backing half way off the back, stopping at the fold.
3. Put the clear side of the clear contact paper on the table, sticky side up.
4. Attach any little torn or cut pieces of art tissue to the sticky contact paper. No glue is necessary. Holiday shapes such as hearts or flowers can also be used. Add any of the listed optional collage items.
5. When the design is complete, pull the remainder of the contact paper backing off.
6. Fold the remaining contact paper over and stick to the design.
7. Take scissors and trim the ragged edges.
8. If desired, punch a hole in the top of the design, add a piece of yarn and hang the artwork in a window or near a light source.

Want to do more?

Cut the finished contact paper design into a heart shape for a pretty Valentine.

Teaching tips

The folding steps can be very wrinkly and off center depending on the ages and abilities of the artists. Accept this outcome.

★ PRESCHOOL ART

Valentine Mice

These mice are great for delivering Valentine messages.

Words to use

mouse
whiskers
nose
tail
greeting

Materials

red paper hearts
black felt pen
bits of string,
   about 3" long
glue

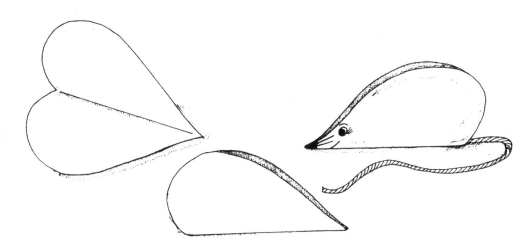

What to do

1. Fold the paper heart in half and find the mouse. The nose and whiskers are at the tapered end—draw them in (see illustration).
2. For the tail, glue the string on the inside of the fold (opposite the end with the nose and whiskers), and let it hang out. There's the mouse!
3. Add a greeting on the inside.

★ EARTHWAYS

Valentine Hearts 3+

Hearts are always popular!

Words to use

elephant ear
symmetrical
doilies

Materials

colored construction paper—red, white and pink
children's scissors (don't forget a pair or two for the lefties)
white glue or glue sticks
paper doilies—these aren't too expensive and add a nice touch
red felt pen

What to do

1. Show the children how to cut hearts on a fold. Fold the paper, and along the fold draw an "elephant's ear." Cut this out on the fold, and you have a symmetrical heart! Vary the size of the elephant's ear to make larger or smaller hearts. This method is much easier than trying to draw the whole heart.
2. Glue different color and size hearts on top of each other, on doilies, etc. Let the children have fun.
3. The teacher can sit and cut lots of different size hearts for the little children to use. You can also be the message writer, if need be—perhaps using a red felt tip pen.

Note: This is also a great time to use saved scraps of fancy wrapping paper, foil papers, etc.

★ EARTHWAYS

Lace Rubbing

4+

Children practice fine motor skills in this activity.

Words to use

lace
design
rub

Materials

jumbo crayons, peeled
scraps of lace, fabric or plastic cut into hearts, squares, circles, strips or any shapes
white drawing paper
masking tape, optional

What to do

1. Select lace shapes and place them on the table. Place a loop of masking tape on the backs of the shapes, if desired, and stick them to the table.
2. Place a sheet of white drawing paper over the shapes. You may tape the corners of the paper to the table to help keep the paper wiggle free.
3. Rub peeled crayons back and forth over the shapes under the paper. A rubbing will emerge.

Want to do more?

Move shapes around, change colors, try new shapes, make greeting cards or cut out shapes to hang in the window or from the ceiling.

Teaching tips

Help the artist draw or trace a heart shape. Children's rubbings are not always like an adult's. Very young children are just learning the idea of rubbings and to control the crayon. Be patient.

★ PRESCHOOL ART

Ladybug's Family   4+

These heart-shaped ladybugs make a cute Valentine's Day card, and the varying sizes allow the children to order them from largest to smallest.

Words to use

card
largest
smallest
size
message

Materials

12" x 9" red and white construction paper rectangles, one of each color per child
non-toxic black markers or black crayons
3" strips of black construction paper approximately 1/4" wide, five per child
glue or glue sticks
scissors
pencils (unsharpened)
crayons
pebbles, optional

9"

② unfold heart shapes, cut strips of black paper for antenna

6"

① cut heart shapes out of red paper

9"

12"

③ complete and attach to white paper

What to do

1. Fold the red construction paper in half and cut out several hearts of varying sizes (see illustration). Show the older children how to draw the half heart on the fold and let them cut out the hearts themselves. These will be the ladybugs' shells.
2. Put black dots on the ladybugs' red shells.

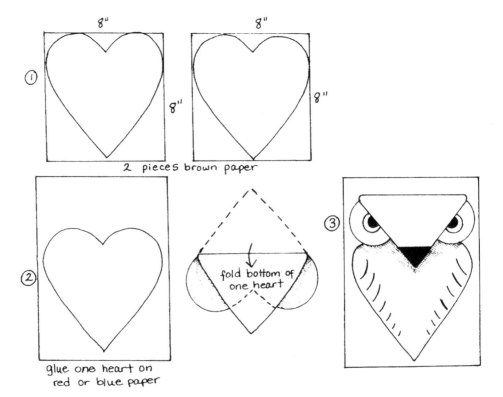

3. Fold the white paper in half to make a card and glue the ladybugs on the front. You could have the children order them from large to small or vice versa. Show the children how to curl the antenna (black strip) by wrapping it around a pencil. Glue one to each ladybug.

4. Write a message inside or allow children to decorate the inside with crayons or more ladybugs. They could have a trail of large to small ladybugs traveling all over the card!

Want to do more?

Ladybugs can also be made from flat pebbles. Collect various sizes with the children, enough so that each child can have his or her own little family. Have the children wash and dry them, paint them red and add small black dots. These could be paperweights or houseplant decorations.

Book to read

Grouchy Lady Bug by Eric Carle

★ THE GIANT ENCYCLOPEDIA OF THEME ACTIVITIES

An Owl Valentine   4+

Children practice fine motor skills while cutting and pasting to make this unusual owl valentine.

Words to use

valentine
heart
cut
fold
owl
eyes
beak
message
lift

Materials

12" x 9" blue or red construction paper, one piece per child

8" x 8" brown construction paper, 2 per child

markers

scissors

glue or glue sticks

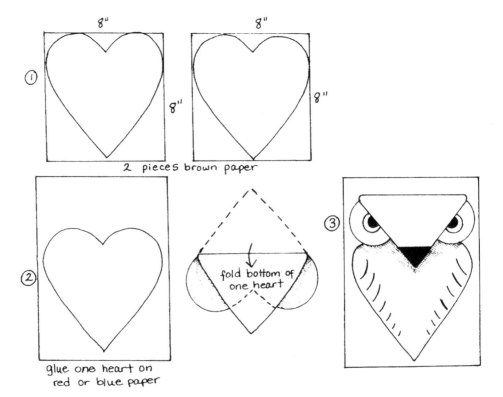

FEBRUARY

art activities

194

What to do

1. On the brown paper, draw and cut out two large heart shapes. They should be the same size. Children may do the cutting.
2. Glue one brown heart on the blue or red paper.
3. Fold the other heart in the center so that the tip covers the top of the heart (see illustration).
4. Glue the folded heart upside down on top of the other heart (see illustration).
5. Draw the eyes and color in the beak with markers.

Want to do more?

Have each child dictate a short Valentine's Day message and write it on the inside folded part of the owl's beak. When you lift the beak, you can see the message.

★ THE GIANT ENCYCLOPEDIA OF THEME ACTIVITIES

Heart a L'art

4+

Hearts fit any which way on this seasonal collage.

Words to use

pattern
stencil
collage

Materials

variety of papers—wrapping paper, magazine pictures, colored paper, tissue paper, posters or book jackets
scissors
glue
matte board or cardboard
crayons, felt pens, paints or any drawing/coloring tools
heart-shaped stencils or patterns

What to do

1. Trace heart-shaped patterns or stencils on any variety of papers or draw hearts free hand.
2. Cut out the shapes. Use the heart-shaped holes left from the hearts too.
3. Begin gluing hearts on the matte board or cardboard in any design or pattern desired.
4. Add drawings with pen or crayon on the matte board too, if desired.
5. Some artists like to fill the entire matte board with hearts, while others prefer a simple approach.

Want to do more?

Use the hearts for Valentine cards, mobiles, posters or wall decorations.

Teaching tips

Hearts are often difficult to draw but are so enjoyed by young children that stencils and patterns are fun to use once in awhile.

★ PRESCHOOL ART

Heart Flutters

Children create heart designs to hang at home or school.

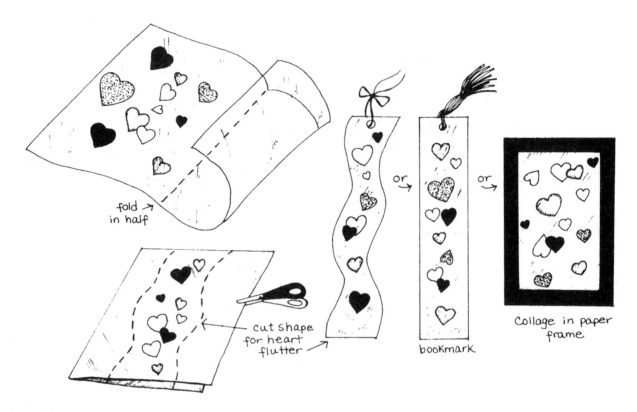

fold
in half

cut shape
for heart
flutter

bookmark

Collage in paper
frame

Words to use

flutter   wax paper
design   hang

Materials

one sheet of wax paper, folded and opened
white glue in a dish, thinned with water until milky (add a few drops of liquid detergent to
    prevent beading)
big paintbrush   art tissue
scissors   newspaper covered table
hole punch   yarn or rubber bands

What to do

1. Brush thinned white glue on half of the wax paper.
2. Stick heart shapes or pieces and patterns of torn or cut art tissue in any colors all over the sticky
    wax paper. Valentine colors would be effective for a fluttery decoration.
3. Brush more white glue over the hearts or tissue designs.
4. Fold the rest of the wax paper over the design.
5. Dry overnight.
6. Cut the dry tissue collage into long skinny shapes or strips—snakes, lightning or other shapes.
7. Punch a hole in the top of each strip.

8. Loop a rubber band or piece of yarn through the hole.
9. Hang the heart flutters from a stick, a hanger or from pins in the frames around a window.

Want to do more?

Make bookmarks instead of flutters. Frame the tissue collage instead of cutting it into strips.

Teaching tips

Punch the hole at least one-third inch from the end to prevent tearing. Expect the wet glue to look cloudy; it will dry clear.

★ Preschool Art

Valentine Swans   5+

This swan is a beautiful way to send a Valentine's message.

Words to use

swan
card
message

Materials

thick white paper or
    card stock (water-
    color paper works
    well), or use white
    drawing paper for
    the swans and
    mount them on a
    piece of red con-
    struction paper
pen or pencil
scissors
white glue or glue
    sticks

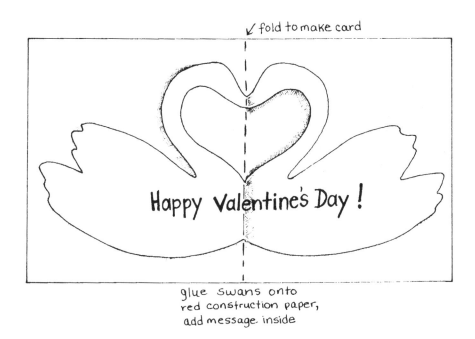

glue swans onto
red construction paper,
add message inside

What to do

1. Fold the paper. Fold the swan pattern (see illustration), place it on the folded edge and trace it onto the paper. The older children may be able to do this. (Enlarge the swan pattern, if desired.)
2. Cut the swans out on the fold (you will be cutting 2 swans at once), helping those children who need it.
3. Open the folded swans. You can write a message inside the fold if you like. If you used lightweight paper for the swans, glue the swans onto red construction paper, fold the paper down the middle of the swans (like a card) and write the message on the inside of the card.

★ Earthways

Circle Time and Group Activities

Groundhog   3+

Teaches children about Groundhog Day.

Words to use

groundhog
hole
ground
cloudy
sunny

Materials

What to do

1. Choose one child to be the groundhog.
2. She rolls herself into a ball and pretends to be inside a hole in the ground.
3. Recite this poem with the children.

> *Groundhog, groundhog, come on out and play.*
> *It's a beautiful, beautiful February day.*
> *The sun is shining and the sky is blue.*
> *Won't you come on out? We want to play with you.*
>   *Jackie Silberg*

4. The groundhog slowly comes out of the hole and looks around.
5. She sees her shadow and says, "Oh dear, there will be six more weeks of winter."
6. Then the groundhog goes back inside her hole.
7. Recite this poem with the children.

> *Groundhog, groundhog, come on out and play.*
> *It's a gloomy, gloomy February day.*
> *The air feels chilly and the sky is gray.*
> *Won't you come on out? We want to play today.*
>   *Jackie Silberg*

8. This time the groundhog comes out and says, "Okay, let's play. I don't see my shadow."

★ 500 FIVE MINUTE GAMES

Color Magic

3+

Teaches children about colors.

Words to use

color words—red, yellow, blue, green, purple
mix
predict
What will happen if...?

Materials

books about colors (see list below)
plastic or glass cups
food coloring (red, yellow, blue, green)
water
spoons to mix colors

What to do

1. Read a book about colors.
2. Say, "Let's see what colors you are wearing today."
3. Sing, "Red stand up, red stand up, red sit down, blue stand up...." Give all children a chance to participate.
4. Say, "We're going to see what happens when we mix colors."
5. Let children take turns mixing food coloring in the water.
6. Ask children what they think will happen if you mix red and yellow, yellow and blue (or any two colors).
7. Mix the two colors that you ask the children about immediately after discussing their predictions, such as mixing red and yellow, blue and yellow.

Want to do more?

Art: Fingerpaint with primary colors. Make colored playdough. What happens when you mix red and yellow or yellow and blue playdough? Celebrate a specific color by asking the children to wear clothes of a specific color during that week. Friday can be Multicolored Day.

Books to read

Growing Colors by Bruce McMillan
Is It Red? Is It Yellow? Is It Blue? by Tana Hoban
Red, Yellow, Blue Shoe by Tana Hoban

★ THE GIANT ENCYCLOPEDIA OF CIRCLE TIME AND GROUP ACTIVITIES

My Favorite Color Chart

3+

Teaches children about graphing.

Words to use

favorite
chart
color word
graph
markers
categorize

Materials

poster board
markers in basic colors

What to do

1. Talk to children about having a favorite color. Explain that favorite means the one you like best and that you like it because you think it is pretty or it makes you feel good.
2. One at a time, write each child's name on the poster board and have them indicate their favorite color. For children who know the names of colors, encourage them to say it. For younger children, ask them to point to the marker of the color they like. Next to each child's name, color a circle or happy face in the color they chose.
3. Display the chart in the classroom.

Want to do more?

Art: Children make a favorite color collage, using crayons, markers, paint, pipe cleaners and other materials that are the color they chose.
Math: Put out different colored objects so that children can categorize favorite colored items. Provide several objects and ask the child which object is missing.

Book to read

The Blue Balloon by Mike Inkpen

Home connection

Send a note home to parents asking them to dress their child the next day in his favorite color.

★ THE GIANT ENCYCLOPEDIA OF CIRCLE TIME AND GROUP ACTIVITIES

Hurry, Hurry, Fire Truck

Teaches children about fire trucks and fire fighters.

Words to use

fire truck
bell
turn
climb

Materials

What to do

Sing the following chant with motions at circle time. Encourage the children to do the motions and then to say the words with you.

"Hurry, Hurry, Drive the Fire Truck"
Hurry, hurry, drive the fire truck (hands on steering wheel)
Hurry, hurry, drive the fire truck,
Hurry, hurry, drive the fire truck,
Ding, ding, ding, ding, ding. (ring bell)

Hurry, hurry, turn the corner, (lean to the right)
Hurry, hurry, turn the corner, (lean to the left)
Hurry, hurry, turn the corner,
Ding, ding, ding, ding, ding. (ring bell)

Other verses:

Hurry, hurry, climb the ladder.... (climb the ladder)
Slowly, slowly, back to the fire station.... (lean slowly to the left and to the right)

★ THE GIANT ENCYCLOPEDIA OF CIRCLE TIME AND GROUP ACTIVITIES

Who Is Wearing Red Today?

3+

Children learn about colors with this activity.

Words to use

wear
clothes

Materials

What to do

1. While children are sitting at circle time, sing the following song to the tune of "Mary Had a Little Lamb."

> *Who is wearing red today,*
> *Red today, red today?*
> *Who is wearing red today?*
> *Please stand up.*

2. Ask the children (one child at a time) to show you where they are wearing the color you asked for.
3. Change the color each time you sing the song, making sure each child gets a turn.

Want to do more?

Game: Play "I Spy" and have the children look around the room for specific colors.
Music: During music time, play Hap Palmer's recording of "What Are You Wearing?" and "Colors."

Books to read

Red Bear by Bodel Rikys
Red, Blue, Yellow Shoe by Tana Hoban

★ THE GIANT ENCYCLOPEDIA OF CIRCLE TIME AND GROUP ACTIVITIES

How Did You Get to School Today?

3+

Children learn about different forms of transportation.

Words to use

bike
shoe
bus
train
car
truck

Materials

outlines cut from white paper (truck, car, train, bus, shoe and bicycle)
crayons or markers
poster board
tape

What to do

1. At circle time ask the children how they traveled to school. Give each child an outline representing his mode of transportation to school.
2. Ask the children to name the color of the vehicle or shoe that they used to get to school. Provide crayons or markers for the children to use in coloring their outlines the appropriate colors.
3. Write the name of each child on their outline and use the outlines to make a class graph of how the children traveled to school. Ask each child to tape his outline in the column on the graph that has the same outline labeling that column. Talk about the different ways that the children traveled to school and compare the number of outlines in each column on the graph.
4. Sing the following song to the tune of "Mary Wore Her Red Dress."

> *Johnny (child's name) took a blue bike, (mode of transportation)*
> *Blue bike, blue bike*
> *Johnny took a blue bike*
> *To get to school today.*

> *The shoe variation is:*
> *Cindy used her purple shoes,*
> *Purple shoes, purple shoes*
> *Cindy used her purple shoes*
> *To get to school today.*

5. Ask the question:

> *Who took a red truck,*
> *Red truck, red truck*
> *Who took a red truck*
> *To get to school today?*

6. Continue singing a version of the song until all the children have been named in the song.

★ The Giant Encyclopedia of Circle Time and Group Activities

Transportation

3+

Teaches children about trains.

Words to use

all aboard	train
station	seats
seats	whistle
wheels	slow
fast	curve
deliver	groceries
food	grocery store

Materials

chairs (1 per child)

What to do

1. Arrange the chairs in a curvy line.
2. Ask the children to sit in a chair and tell them that the train is about to leave. Blow a whistle, calling, "All aboard! Train is leaving! All aboard!"
3. Sing the following song:

> *I'm a train, I'm a train*
> *I'm a choo-choo train.*
> *I ride in the sun.*
> *I ride in the rain.*
> *My wheels go slow.*
> *It depends, it depends*
> *On where I go.*
> *Chugga, chugga, chugga (continue going faster and faster)*
> *Choo! Choo!*

4. Tell the children that the train is going to deliver food to grocery stores and the train will travel up mountains and down mountains. Emphasize that there are lots of curvy and bouncy tracks for the train to ride over. Repeat the song, being animated and enthusiastic. (As the train goes uphill, lean back and chug slowly. As the train goes downhill, lean forward and chug fast. On the curvy track, lean left or right, exaggerating the chug-g-g bounce too.)
5. At the end of the train ride, tell the children that the train has arrived at a grocery store and they should get off the train and sit in a circle on the carpet.
6. Talk with the children about the train ride. Ask the children what groceries the train brought to the grocery store. Explain that groceries are often carried by train and then loaded into trucks to be delivered to the grocery stores.

Book to read

The Caboose Who Got Loose by Bill Peet

★ THE GIANT ENCYCLOPEDIA OF CIRCLE TIME AND GROUP ACTIVITIES

Road, Sky or Water

3+

Children learn to classify types of transportation according to where they are used (for example: airplanes—in the sky, trucks—on roadways).

Words to use

boat
airplane
car
truck

Materials

pictures or models of boats, airplanes, cars and trucks

What to do

1. Make signs with illustrations for "Road," "Sky" and "Water."
2. Talk to the children about different modes of transportation.
3. Show the children the signs and the pictures or models of boats, airplanes, cars and trucks.
4. Ask the children under which sign each picture or model should go, and place it there.

Want to do more?

Let children play with toy boats in the water table or with cars and trucks in the sand table.

Books to read

Mike Mulligan and His Steam Shovel by V.L. Burton
Round Trip by A. Jonas
Cars and Trucks and Things That Go by Richard Scarry

★ THE GIANT ENCYCLOPEDIA OF THEME ACTIVITIES

How Do I Get There?

3+

Children practice identifying and discussing various modes of transportation by guessing the identity of toy vehicles in a grab bag.

Words to use

travel
guess

Materials

puppet
large bag
various toy vehicles, such as helicopter, train, airplane, car, truck, motorcycle, boat, rocketship or horse

What to do

1. Put all the toys in the bag.
2. Introduce the puppet: "My friend has a problem. He needs to go to _____. How can he get there?" Let children name different ways the puppet can travel. Ask if they will be good ways to travel. Why or why not?
3. Show the bag. Explain that inside the bag are ways that we can travel, and that the word we use is transportation. This is how we get from one place to another.
4. Describe a mode of transportation that you have in the bag. Have the children make guesses. When it is correctly named, remove the toy from the bag. Continue until all toys are named.

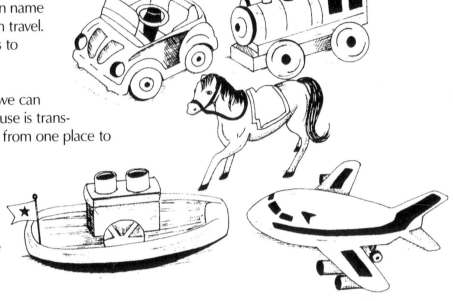

Want to do more?

Sort the toys as to whether they are ways to travel by air, land or water. Play the song "Sammy" by Hap Palmer on the Getting to Know Myself album. Show pictures of each animal/insect in the song. How does it move? Have the children move according to the song.

Song to sing

"This Is the Way We Row a Boat" sung to the tune of "Here We Go 'Round the Mulberry Bush"

> *This is the way we row a boat,*
> *Row a boat, row a boat.*
> *This is the way we row a boat,*
> *Early in the morning.*
>
> *This is the way we fly a plane...*
> *Drive a car...*
> *Ride a horse....*

★ THE GIANT ENCYCLOPEDIA OF THEME ACTIVITIES

Airplane Song and Activities

4+

Teaches children about airplane travel.

Words to use

airplane   fly
seat belt   luggage

Materials

What to do

1. At circle time sing "The Airplane Song" to the tune of "The Wheels of the Bus."

> *The pilot on the airplane says fasten your belts (fasten seat belts)*
> *Fasten your belts, fasten your belts.*
> *The pilot on the airplane says fasten your belts*
> *When flying through the sky.*

Additional verses:

> *The children on the airplane go bumpity bump... (move up and down)*
> *The babies on the airplane go waa, waa... (rub eyes and pretend to cry)*
> *The signs on the airplane go ding, ding, ding... (point to signs)*
> *The drinks on the airplane go splish, splash, splish... (pretend to hold a glass and move it)*
> *The luggage on the plane goes up and down... (pretend to be luggage going up and down)*

2. At the end of the song, say, "We have now reached our destination. You may unbuckle your seat belts!"
3. Ask the children to name other things on an airplane that you could add to the song. Write additional verses with the children.

Want to do more?

Dramatic play: Set up an airplane in the classroom with chairs and headphones (from listening center) for the pilot and copilot who sit in the first two chairs. Ask the children to name their destination. The flight attendants serve food (from the housekeeping center) on trays. Babies (dolls) are welcome as long as they are accompanied by an adult (child). Luggage should be stored under the seat.

Language: Children write and illustrate stories of their flight in the dramatic play area or imagine a place where they would like to fly if they could go anywhere in the world. Compile their papers and make a class book.

Science: Make paper airplanes and fly the planes inside, outside, from the top of stairs and near a fan. Ask the children to measure and record the distance each plane travels. The distance can be graphed to help the children compare the differences in distance.

★ THE GIANT ENCYCLOPEDIA OF CIRCLE TIME AND GROUP ACTIVITIES

FEBRUARY

circle time activities

Won or Two

4+

Children may respond to this activity in several ways: the recipient may promptly consume the cookie; the cookie may be accepted and divided and a portion returned to the original giver; the cookie may be given only after considerable negotiation. This activity teaches children generosity, kindness and sharing, as well as problem-solving skills.

Words to use

problem solving
partner
generous
consideration

Materials

one napkin per pair of children
one nutritious cookie (or other food) for each child

What to do

1. Ask the children to wash their hands thoroughly. When they are ready for circle time, tell them you have cookies to give them. Tell them, however, that they will have to find a partner and solve a problem first. Once everyone has a partner, ask them to sit facing each other around the circle.
2. Place the napkins between the pairs of children. Put one cookie on one partner's napkin. Ask the children not to touch the cookie yet. Explain, "Here is the problem. The rule is that you can only get the cookie if your partner gives it to you. You cannot take it for yourself." Remind the children of this guideline if they forget.
3. Ask them to begin. Remind them that they cannot take the cookie for themselves. When all the cookies have been given away, put out a second cookie for each pair.
4. Ask the children how they solved the problem. Emphasize the cooperation that took place.
5. If someone has been left without a cookie, consider giving one to them and thanking them for their generosity.

Want to do more?

Use small inexpensive trinkets and other giveaways instead of cookies. Begin with two different food items placed on the napkin.

Book to read

Full Moon Soup by Alastaire Graham

Home connection

Emphasize to parents the importance of getting children to think about conflict resolution rather than simply following through with adult suggestions. They can encourage children to become confident problem solvers. Engage them in brainstorming many possible solutions to a conflict. Once this pool of ideas is created, then begin choosing a solution.

★ THE PEACEFUL CLASSROOM

Dramatic Play Activities

Ship Ahoy

3+

Encourages dramatic play while the children are playing outside.

Words to use

rowboat
fish

Materials

small rowboat
shovel or sandbags

What to do

1. Obtain a small rowboat that is no longer used in the water.
2. Place the boat in the play yard and stabilize it so that it is level and doesn't rock. (This can be done by placing it in a small trench and/or placing sand or sandbags around the sides.)
3. Children "drive" the boat or "fish" at will.
4. The boat may become a permanent or temporary addition to the playground equipment.

★ THE INSTANT CURRICULUM

Box Cars and Boats

3+

Encourages the children to use their imagination.

Words to use

imagination
This box could be a ...

Materials

medium to large size boxes

What to do

1. At various times, bring medium to large size boxes into the room for children to use as they wish. Boxes should be big enough for children to sit in.
2. A one-child box might become a car, and a long box might become a canoe for two.
3. Children might place a series of boxes in a line to make a train.

★ THE INSTANT CURRICULUM

Fill'er Up and Fix'er Up!

3+

This activity helps children begin to think about the fact that cars and machines need care and maintenance. Having a service station set up near the wheel toys also offers play opportunities to the children waiting for a turn on the wheel toys.

Words to use

mechanic
broken
fix
pump
hose
service station
gas
money
cash register
customer
attendant

Materials

a gas pump (with the children, you can make a gas pump by attaching a rubber or plastic hose to a long cylindrical box and painting numerals in a "window" near the top)
play money
cash register
lengths of hose to drive over and to use as air hoses
a rag for wiping windows

What to do

1. The service station should be set up convenient to the tricycle riding area or paths.
2. You could have a box or area actually representing the station and mechanic work area, or just some gas pumps.
3. The two main roles are those of the station attendant and the customer. The customer can tell the attendant what he wants done: "Fill'er up." The attendant can ask, "Check your oil?"

Want to do more?

A customer could also bring an ailing vehicle to the garage for repairs. Add mechanics' tools and wrenches or facsimiles. If the children don't seem to be thinking of much on their own, you could fill a useful role as a customer, asking for assistance and requesting various services. "It has trouble starting. Do you think I need a new battery?" "My car broke down over there on the freeway. Can you come and get it and fix it for me?"

FEBRUARY

dramatic play activities

Fire! 3+

In this activity the children are acting out scary situations while feeling a greater sense of control. They may also begin to understand the role of the fire department in a community.

Words to use

alarm
siren
fire

Materials

decorate a tricycle to look like a fire engine
bell or siren (voices)
pieces of hose
fire hats
jackets, large boots, whatever else you can scrounge
orange and yellow paper flames, optional

What to do

1. If props are there (and sometimes even if they're not) the children are likely to play "fire" spontaneously.
2. If you have a "volunteer" force, you could sound the siren or ring the bell, and other members of the "department," occupied in their "usual work" elsewhere on the playground, would have to stop what they are doing and rush over to the fire station to assemble and drive the vehicle to the scene of the fire.

Want to do more?

A visit to the local fire department or a visit by a fire truck to the center would inspire the children. This would be an ideal time to teach the "drop and roll" technique to the children. Also drill the children on how to call the fire department and what to tell them.

★ THE OUTSIDE PLAY AND LEARNING BOOK

Pretend Bus 3+

Children will use their knowledge of a song and their imagination in this activity.

Words to use

bus
driver
money
seats

FEBRUARY

dramatic play activities

211

Materials

bus props—bus driver cap, pretend money, a bowl or pan for the money, chairs arranged in rows of two, newspaper, baby dolls, etc.

What to do

Provide the props and encourage the children to act out the situations in the song, "The Wheels on the Bus."

★ WHERE IS THUMBKIN?

Space Helmets   3+

There are many concepts to be learned from outer space, yet in reality few of us will ever get there. Right? Wrong! We can get there in a few seconds if we are properly prepared. This activity gets the children into a proper frame of mind and prepares them for the delightful fantasy of journeying into space.

Words to use

helmet
space
astronaut
space shuttle
planets
stars
moon
gravity
launch

← add decoration to "helmet"

cut milk jug along dotted line

Materials

1 gallon plastic milk jugs
masking tape or duct tape
miscellaneous pieces of decorative
    material (for example, strips of
    colored transparent plastic from term paper covers, pipe cleaners, garbage bag ties, bread tags, bits of Styrofoam)
white glue
razor blade or box cutter (for adult use only)
permanent markers
scissors

What to do

1. Using a razor blade or sharp scissors, cut the space helmet from the milk jug in the shape shown in the illustration.
Note: This step should be done by an adult. Cover all sharp edges with masking tape or duct tape.
2. Decorate the helmet with objects from the materials suggested. Use white glue as needed.

212

Younger children will probably need lots of help, but it will be worth it for the fun they'll have with the completed helmet. Cutting and decorating should be done in one session and the helmets set aside to dry thoroughly.

3. When the helmets are dry, the children can become space pioneers off to explore the far reaches of the galaxy.

Want to do more?

Space fantasies are fun to act out. Select a planet to visit or talk about travel to the moon. Build a space traveling machine from a large box. Allow each child a chance to visit another planet. Talk about the weightlessness and the absence of air to breathe. Talk about the differences between real space exploration, such as the space shuttle launches, and fantasy travel a la Star Wars and E.T. Bring in books and magazines about space travel and outer space.

★ MUDPIES TO MAGNETS

Favorite Color Day   3+

Children learn to sort clothing by colors.

Words to use

favorite
match
sort

Materials

full length mirror
dress-up clothes
paper bags
construction paper
stapler

What to do

1. Staple sheets of construction paper in primary and secondary colors to paper grocery bags.
2. Let the children who select the housekeeping center during free play sort the clothing by color by placing the garments into the appropriate paper bag.
3. During clean-up time, leave the clothes in the bags and the next day, have the children sort them by other characteristics such as clothes with snaps, zippers and buttons, or adult, children and baby clothes, or blouses, shirts, pants and dresses.

Teaching tips

Many good activities for young children combine more than one area of the curriculum. Younger children may need to sort by fewer colors and older children may be able to sort by two simple attributes, such as color and whether the garment is adult, child or baby clothing.

★ MORE STORY S-T-R-E-T-C-H-E-R-S

dramatic play activities

Putting Children to Bed   3+

Children learn to arrange the housekeeping corner for bedtime activities that take place in a family.

Words to use

bedtime
goodnight
lullaby

Materials

Sloppy Kisses by Elizabeth Winthrop
dolls
stuffed animals
bedroom furniture
blankets
pillows
kitchen appliances
table
utensils

What to do

1. Show the pictures in *Sloppy Kisses* of the family eating together and then of the children being tucked in and saying "goodnight."
2. Ask the children about the routines of their family from dinner time through going to bed.
3. Have one child show his family routine by putting a doll or stuffed animal to bed. Ask what happens first, second, next. If the child's parent reads a book, have the child read or pretend to read a book. If the child's parent sings a lullaby, ask the child to sing the lullaby.
4. Let other children tell more about what their families do, then ask the players to pretend they are a family and it is bedtime for the children.
5. Leave the players to change and improvise the roles on their own.

★ MORE STORY S-T-R-E-T-C-H-E-R-S

Baskets for Groceries   3+

Children practice problem-solving skills while making these useful baskets.

Words to use

basket
hold
contain
purchase

Materials

cardboard boxes such as shoe
  boxes
markers and crayons
pipe cleaners

What to do

1. Construct grocery baskets
   using cardboard boxes.
2. Ask the children to decorate
   the containers and attach pipe
   cleaners for the handles.
3. Use these child-size baskets
   when the children are making
   purchases and checking out of
   the grocery store.

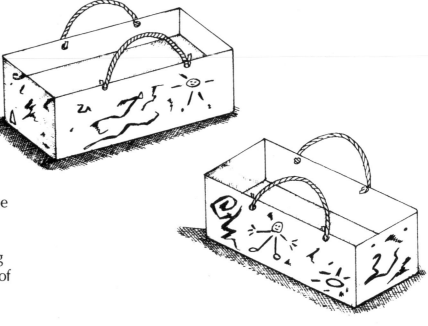

★ THE COMPLETE LEARNING CENTER BOOK

The Dark Place   3+

Creating a dark space helps children learn to overcome their fear of the dark.

Words to use

dark
light
glow-in-the-dark

Materials

black shade cloth
tape
black paper
glow-in-the-dark stickers

What to do

1. Create a dark place in the corner of the Nighttime Center by taping pieces of black shade cloth
   across one corner of the center. The fabric will let some light into the area so it will not be too dark.
2. Put black paper on the walls of the center. Place glow-in-the-dark star stickers in the dark area.
3. Allowing the children to help create the dark space will make it less frightening and will help them
   be more courageous when they are using the corner. The children enter and leave this section of
   the center whenever they choose.

★ THE COMPLETE LEARNING CENTER BOOK

dramatic play activities

Language Activities

Truck Sounds

3+

Children learn to make the sound effects of a truck.

Words to use

engine
honk
beep
screech
sounds

Materials

Truck Song by Diane Siebert
tape recorder
cassette tapes

What to do

1. Read *Truck Song* and ask the children to make some of the sound effects they make when they are playing with the trucks in the block building area. They can make engine noises, the sounds of warning when trucks are backing up, the screeching of brakes and the beeping of horns. Look at the illustrations of the truck driving through rain and think of sound effects: the swishing of the water under the tires and the slapping of the windshield wipers.
2. Practice the sounds a few times.
3. Tape record yourself reading *Truck Song* with the children providing the sound effects.
4. Add the tape and the book to the collection for the listening station. You'll find the children's favorite selections are the ones they helped to record.

Teaching tips

If you have access to a real truck from one of the parents, tape record the sound of the brakes, the air horn, the backing-up warning sound, the windshield wipers slapping and some CB messages.

★ STORY S-T-R-E-T-C-H-E-R-S

Vehicles

Children learn about the different types of vehicles.

Words to use

car/road   bus/road
train/track   subway/track
airplane/sky

Materials

several kinds of toy vehicles
photos or pictures that relate to each vehicle, for example, train/tracks, rocket/moon, car/garage, boat/ocean, etc.

What to do

Encourage the children to match vehicles to related pictures.

★ Where Is Thumbkin?

Our Favorite Bedtime Books

3+

Children learn to select a favorite bedtime book.

Words to use

bedtime   nap time
nighttime   relax
sleep

Materials

Daddy Makes the Best Spaghetti by Anna Grossnickle Hines
collection of books about bedtime, nap time, nighttime or family experiences

What to do

1. Show the illustrations from *Daddy Makes the Best Spaghetti* where the little boy and his father are listening to his mother read a bedtime story.
2. Read one of your favorite bedtime or nap time books in a lowered, calm voice. Talk with the children about how you relax when you read the book.
3. Ask the children to bring a book from home, one of their favorite books that helps them relax and go to sleep.
4. During the week, select bedtime books to read aloud in the library corner and at times during the day when a relaxing mood is needed.

Teaching tips

If some of your children have few books at home, let these children go with you to the school or city library and check out books for the rest of the class.

★ More Story S-t-r-e-t-c-h-e-r-s

FEBRUARY

language activities

Writing a Nighttime Walking Adventure

3+

Children learn to express in writing a real or imaginary walk.

Words to use

writing
owling
going for a walk

Materials

Owl Moon by Jane Yolen
an assortment of writing papers and
    instruments

What to do

1. Read *Owl Moon* to the children and discuss with a small group of children how they might feel on an imaginary owling walk. Ask the children to recall any nighttime walks they have taken and how they felt. How was it different from or like the walk in *Owl Moon*.
2. Encourage the children to write about an imaginary walk where they are looking for something special or where something surprises them.
3. Let the children choose writing partners or write on their own if they so choose.

Teaching tips

With younger children, write for them as they describe their imaginary walks. Let them watch as you transform their spoken ideas into written language, which you can then read back to them. Remember, too, that writing is a process that takes time. Allow the older children long writing periods without ringing bells to change activities every fifteen or twenty minutes.

★ MORE STORY S-T-R-E-T-C-H-E-R-S

Experience Charts

3+

This is an opportunity for children to describe events and see them transcribed into written form.

Words to use

words   say
write   describe

Matrials

chart tablet and marker

What to do

1. Encourage children to describe an experience or their feelings about an experience.
2. Write them on a chart as children describe them orally, such as:

> We went to the barn.
> We saw cows and horses.
> We played in the hay.
> The hay smelled good.

★ THE INSTANT CURRICULUM

Name Game

3+

Encourages children's rhyming skills.

Words to use

rhyme   sounds like

Materials

What to do

1. During the day when it's necessary to call a child's name, use a teachable moment for children to learn rhyming sounds.
2. Say, "Would the child whose name rhymes with TOY sit down for snack?"
3. Roy or Joy or any other person with a name that rhymes responds to the request.

★ THE INSTANT CURRICULUM

Broken Names

3+

Encourages children to recognize their names.

Words to use

puzzle   piece
back together

Materials

large cards   marker
scissors

What to do

1. Write each child's name on a large card.
2. Cut the card into puzzle pieces, making each letter a puzzle piece.
3. Children put the letters back together to spell their names correctly.
4. Make the name cards self-correcting by making each cut between letters different.

★ THE INSTANT CURRICULUM

New Words

4+

This activity encourages the development of memory skills.

Words to use

sounds   new

Materials

chart tablet paper
crayon or marker

What to do

1. Talk about sounds that could go with the song, The Wheels on the Bus. For example, the wipers on the bus go squeak, squeak, squeak or the money on the bus goes jingle, jingle, jingle.
2. Write the sounds on the chart tablet paper.
3. Sing the song with new verses.

★ WHERE IS THUMBKIN?

Funny Funny Papers

4+

Children learn to make up their own stories.

Words to use

story   pictures
write

Materials

comic strips   white tape or white-out
pencil or pen

What to do

1. Provide each child with a comic strip with the words in the strip blanked out. (White-out works well.)
2. Let the children create their own version of the story by telling the story they see in the pictures.
3. Dictated stories can be written by the teacher in the blanked out spaces so that children develop the concept that writing is talk written down.

★ THE INSTANT CURRICULUM

FEBRUARY

language activities

Star Wishes

4+

Encourages children's creative thinking.

Words to use

wish
write
star

Materials

paper stars
pencil or pen

What to do

1. Ask the children to think about a wish they would make on a star.
2. The children dictate their wishes and record them on paper stars.
3. Use for bulletin board decorations.

★ WHERE IS THUMBKIN?

Treasure Hunt

4+

The children must listen to verbal directions and do some reasoning. Vocabulary and space words, as well as measuring concepts, could be emphasized, depending on the clues.

Words to use

treasure   hunt
hide   find

Materials

some "treasure" to hide
paper and pencil for clues

What to do

1. Hide a treasure on the playground (gold painted rocks, morning snack).
2. Give the children a series of clues, one at a time, leading to the treasure.
3. The children must find each clue, which has directions to lead them to the next clue, and finally to the treasure.

Want to do more?

With younger children, the adult could go along and be there to read the next clue when the children find it. The clues should be very simple, using vocabulary they know. For example, the next clue is under the window on the inside of the playhouse. Make the game more and more complex for older children. You could involve measuring, using a compass and figuring out riddles.

★ THE OUTSIDE PLAY AND LEARNING BOOK

language activities

Math Activities

Counting Cars, Vans, Trucks, Buses

3+

Children practice counting.

Words to use

cars
vans
trucks
buses
vehicle
transportation
sort
categories
count
How many...?

Materials

a variety of small toy vehicles
The Car Trip by Helen Oxenbury, optional

What to do

1. Invite the children to bring their little toy cars, trucks, vans and buses to school.
2. Label the toys on the morning that they are brought in so that there will be no confusion about who the owners are.
3. Create a display of all the vehicles at the mathematics table.
4. Have the children put the vehicles into categories: cars, several different types of trucks from paneled trucks to eighteen wheelers, vans for pleasure and those for deliveries, school buses and city buses.
5. Practice counting by counting the vehicles in each category.

Teaching tips

Recall that counting is one way we entertain ourselves when we have a long car ride. We count the number of red cars we see, or big trucks, or cars like ours, or trucks like Grandpa's.

★ STORY S-T-R-E-T-C-H-E-R-S

Sorting

3

Encourages the development of classification and sorting skills.

Words to use

different
same
alike
sort
chart

Materials

empty food containers
plastic grocery cart or basket
laminated chart
markers

What to do

1. Place many different kinds of empty food containers in a plastic grocery cart or a basket.
2. Encourage the children to classify the items by placing the foods that are alike together.
3. A variation of this activity is for children to sort the foods based on their own food preferences: foods they like and foods they don't like.
4. Place a laminated chart on a table for the children to use as they determine food preferences.

★ THE COMPLETE LEARNING CENTER BOOK

Sorting Stars

3+

Children learn visual discrimination skills.

Words to use

size
color
sort

Materials

construction paper
scissors

What to do

1. Cut stars of different sizes and colors.
2. The children sort the stars by color and by size.

★ WHERE IS THUMBKIN?

FEBRUARY

math activities

School Map Puzzle   4+

This activity helps young children build their first map, of a place they know and see every day. Precise map making is not the object. Our purpose is to show that maps exist, that children can make them, and that they represent real places.

Words to use

map
far
near
around
next to
beside
north
south
east
west
orient
location
direction

Materials

paper
glue
crayons or markers
scissors

What to do

1. Draw a large picture of the school yard. On the map, place the big items such as the building, the fence, major trees, sidewalks.
2. With the children, choose the most prominent spots in the yard—slide, tires, swings, and so on—and locate where they are on the map.
3. The children draw the objects on paper and cut them out.
4. Orient the map, putting it at the true, cardinal direction. It is best if you can do this outside where the real objects are.
5. Glue the pictures on the map, checking on the placement by looking at the school yard.

Want to do more?

Make a map of another yard, the park, the school, a school room. Have the parents help the children make a map of their rooms at home. Then they could bring the room maps for story time.

★ MORE MUDPIES TO MAGNETS

Train Sequence

4

Children learn number recognition and sequencing skills.

Words to use

numeral
train car
smallest
largest

Materials

construction paper train cars
construction paper engine and caboose
sticky dots or marker

What to do

1. Place dots or numerals on train cars.
2. The children arrange the cars from smallest numeral or number of dots to largest numeral or number of dots.

★ WHERE IS THUMBKIN?

Music and Movement Activities

Giants and Elves

3+

This activity helps children learn about loud and soft tones.

Words to use

loud   soft
tiptoe   stomp
elf   giant

Materials

drum

What to do

1. Using a drum, beat loudly and softly, while children walk around the room.
2. Children tiptoe like elves to soft music and stomp like giants to loud music.

★ THE INSTANT CURRICULUM

Variations on Old Time Favorites

3+

*Children learn to use familiar songs in new ways,
while developing gross motor skills.*

Words to use

tune
new words

Materials

What to do

Adapt familiar songs to make them appropriate for teaching objectives or to individualize them for your classroom. For example sing "Touch and Stretch" to the tune of "Here We Go 'Round the Mulberry Bush.".

> *verse 1: This is the way I touch my toes, touch my toes, touch my toes.
> This is the way I touch my toes and that's the way it goes."*

> *verse 2: Stretch up high—touch the sky, etc.*

★ THE INSTANT CURRICULUM

Sing and Listen

Develops children's listening skills.

Words to use

record
sing
listen

Materials

tape recorder and blank tape

What to do

1. Record children's voices with the tape recorder as they sing.
2. Re-play for the children to hear.
3. The teacher can add interest by having each child say his name into the recorder before the song.

★ The Instant Curriculum

Twin Tunes

3+

Develops children's listening skills.

Words to use

sing
melody
tune
same

Materials

What to do

1. Have half of the class sing, "Twinkle, Twinkle, Little Star," while the other half listens.
2. Then let the other half of the class sing the "A-B-C Song."
3. Alternate singing and listening.
4. Have both sides sing at the same time, noting that the tunes are the same.

★ The Instant Curriculum

FEBRUARY

music & movement activities

227

Preschool Limbo   3+

Children learn about rhythm.

Words to use

under
bend

Materials

record player or tape
   player
record or tape with limbo
   or Caribbean melody

What to do

1. Play a record with a
   limbo or Caribbean
   melody.
2. Children move rhyth-
   mically around the room in a line, going under a broomstick stretched across two chairs.
3. Children should bend forward, instead of backward, for safety.

← children should bend
   forward for safety

★ THE INSTANT CURRICULUM

Let's Travel   3+

Teaches children about different forms of travel.

Words to use

bus   boat
train   horse

Materials

What to do

1. Talk about different modes of transportation.
2. Sing songs about each mode, for example:

> *The Wheels on the Bus*
> *Row, Row, Row Your Boat*
> *I've Been Working on the Railroad*
> *She'll Be Coming 'Round the Mountain*

★ 500 FIVE MINUTE GAMES

Wheels on the Bus

3+

Children practice thinking skills.

Words to use

wheel
bus
actions
move

Materials

What to do

1. This game offers a different way to sing the popular children's song "The Wheels on the Bus."
2. Sing it all the way through, acting it out as usual.
3. Sing it again, but act out the motions without singing the words.
4. For example, do not sing "'round and 'round," just move your hands in a circular motion.
5. Continue performing the actions without singing the words.
6. This requires a lot of concentration and thinking.

★ 500 FIVE MINUTE GAMES

Obstacle Course

3+

As children move through an obstacle course, they absorb the concepts of space and location words. These concepts are enhanced if an adult is describing what the children are doing.

Words to use

obstacle	over
under	around
through	

Materials

tires	saw horses
ladders	tunnels
planks	yarn
climber	

What to do

1. Moveable materials on the playground, such as tires, saw horses, ladders, tunnels and planks, can be rearranged in conjunction with the climber. Use whatever you have.
2. The things you and the children arrange should be stable and not pose potential safety hazards. If desired, mark out a trail using a long piece of yarn for the children to follow.

Want to do more?

This could be rearranged every day to provide new challenges. Let the children suggest where to put things.

★ THE OUTSIDE PLAY AND LEARNING BOOK

Pussy Willow   3+

Teaches children the scale.

Words to use

scale
notes

Materials

What to do

1. Each line of this poem is sung on a different note of the scale, beginning with "do" as in do, re, mi, fa, sol, la, ti, do.

> *I have a little pussy, (do)*
> *Her fur is silver gray. (re)*
> *She lives down in the meadow (mi)*
> *Not very far away. (fa)*
> *She'll always be a pussy, (sol)*
> *She'll never be a cat. (la)*
> *For she's a pussy willow. (ti)*
> *Now what do you think of that! (do)*
> *Meow, meow, meow, meow, meow,*
> *   meow, meow, meow.*
> *(sing back down the scale, one meow*
> *   for each note)*
> *SCAT!!*

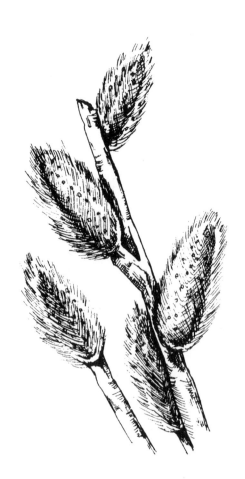

★ 500 FIVE MINUTE GAMES

Body Part Matching   3+

This is a listening activity. The children must hear the words, "you stop," as well as the part of the body you call out. It is also good for developing body awareness.

Words to use

parts of the body
beat
drum
listen

Materials

a drum, optional

What to do

1. Beat the drum while you chant, "You walk, and you walk, and you walk and you stop!" (Vary how may times you repeat, "you walk.")
2. While you do this, the children should walk around in a random way (as opposed to walking in a circle). After you say "stop," call out a body part. Ankles! The children must then touch that part of their body to the same part of the body of someone else.

★ THE OUTSIDE PLAY AND LEARNING BOOK

Science Activities

Flashlights

3+

Children learn how different flashlights give off different amounts of light.

Words to use

light
flashlight
shine
dark
filter
chart
amount of light
bright light
low light
light beam
narrow beam
wide beam

Materials

collection of flashlights
basket
large appliance box and scissors
chart paper

What to do

1. Cut holes in the top of the appliance box so light will filter inside and make the area less frightening.
2. Collect different sizes and shapes of flashlights and place them in a basket outside the entrance to a large appliance box.
3. The children select a flashlight and go inside the dark box to determine the amount of light that flashlight produces.
4. Post a chart with drawings of the different flashlights on the side of the appliance box.
5. At the top of the chart write, "Which flashlight would you use on a dark night?"
6. Ask the children to mark which flashlight they would use.

★ THE COMPLETE LEARNING CENTER BOOK

Listening for the Horses

Encourages children to develop listening skills.

Words to use

ear   listen
ground   hear

Materials

table

What to do

1. Ask the children if they have ever seen someone in a movie put an ear to the ground to find out if horses are coming.
2. Explain that sound carries through the ground and through other materials, such as table tops. The sound also sounds louder.
3. Have two children sit at opposite ends of a long table and take turns scratching under the table. Have one child put her ear on the table while the other child scratches under the table. They will note how much louder the scratching sound is.
4. A further use (and also a good group management technique) is to have children put their heads down on the table to listen for teacher's "scratching signal" to go to lunch, go to circle, etc.

★ THE INSTANT CURRICULUM

Air Pushers

3+

Children learn about the properties of air.

Words to use

push
air
move

Materials

small items, such as paper, feathers or Styrofoam packaging chips
masking tape
empty plastic catsup, mustard or detergent bottles

What to do

1. Place small items, such as paper, feathers or Styrofoam packaging chips in a circle of masking tape on the floor.
2. Let the children take turns trying to "squirt" (push with air) the items out of the circle with empty plastic catsup, mustard or detergent dispensers.

★ THE INSTANT CURRICULUM

Raisin Elevators

3+

Children learn about carbonation.

Words to use

carbonation
bubbles
raisins

Materials

a clear glass
clear carbonated water
4-5 raisins

What to do

1. Pour clear carbonated soda water into a clear glass.
2. Drop four or five raisins into the glass.
3. After 40 to 60 seconds, children will observe raisins moving up and down in the glass.
4. Teacher should help children draw the conclusion that the air bubbles caused the upward movement.
5. Let children observe the glass later in the day when the carbonation has ceased. This will reinforce the role of the air bubbles in lifting the raisins.

★ THE INSTANT CURRICULUM

The Great Air Machine Race

3+

Air takes up space, can move objects and do work. It is, however, a most difficult concept to explain to young children. So, let's look at air as a mover of things. You still can't see it, but an invisible gust can push an object across the table as surely as your finger. With the air machine your children can feel the force of air, see it move things and become skilled enough to move obstacles around or hit a target.

Words to use

air   blow
squeeze   invisible
force   wind
roll   gust

Materials

heavy duty resealable bags
2 sponges for each bag
plastic straws
duct tape

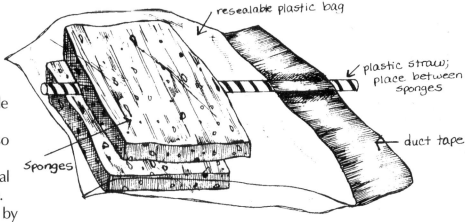

resealable plastic bag

*plastic straw;
place between
sponges*

duct tape

Sponges

What to do

1. Place the sponges inside the bag. Put the straw between the sponges so that it sticks out of the bag (see illustration). Seal the bag with duct tape. The air machine works by squeezing the sponge which should cause a stream of air to be sent out through the straw.
2. Show the children how to work the machine.
3. Give each child a crayon, acorn or other "rollable" object which is to be placed on the table and moved by air only.
4. The Great Air Machine Race now begins as children roll their items across the table.

Want to do more?

Along with the air machine, give each child a set of objects with different shapes. Which shapes are easiest to move? Move pieces of similar shape but different weight. Prepare machines with different sizes or numbers of straws. Try to move small plastic and metal cars with wheels to see which (light vs. heavier) is fastest. Make a soap mixture and blow bubbles.

★ MUDPIES TO MAGNETS

Rampin' It   3+

Ask the children to bring their toy cars and assorted mobile toys to school. Add materials to create appropriate ramps, and the race is on. But it is not easy to produce a good racing ramp. Some will be too low, some too high, and some, after a bit of experimenting, will be just right. Then it is time to test the track with different vehicles, and this is where another set of experiments begins.

Words to use

ramp	change
fastest	slowest
experiment	height
distance	acceleration
friction	speed
force	heavier
lighter	mass

Materials

blocks
small cars and other
   vehicles
books
board—at least 8" wide
   (back of wallpaper
   sample book works
   well)

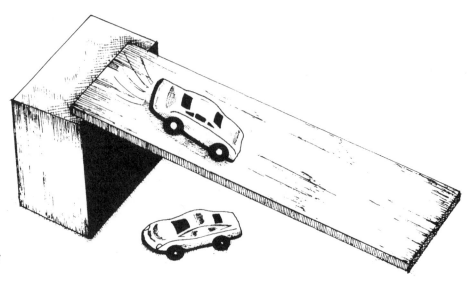

What to do

1. In the block area, or
   another space where
   cars can roll freely,
   show the children how
   to build a ramp. To
   begin with, use the
   board and just one
   block. Let those par-
   ticipating roll their cars down the ramp. Show the children how to hold the cars at the top of the
   ramp and let go without a push. You want to see how far the ramp makes them go without our
   help. After a few trials, the children will probably begin to compare the cars for speed. Explore this
   with them, asking "Which do you think is our fastest car? Our slowest?" Stressing which is the
   class's "best" will help limit the "my car is better" talk.
2. Ask how the ramp could be changed to make the cars travel farther. Let them experiment. They
   may be cautious types who add on one block at a time. They may add as many blocks as possible.
   Encourage problem solving. For example, the ramp is so high that the board keeps slipping off.
   What can we do to keep this from happening? (One group of threes tried to tape it at the bottom
   and prop it with chairs before deciding to take turns holding it. A group of fives just took the top
   block off, saying "that's as high as it goes!") Again, as they build, encourage trial runs with the cars
   to compare distance and/or speed.
3. Some children may want to do formal trials with the ramp at various heights. The distance the cars
   travel can be marked on the floor with tape so that comparisons can be made. What is the best
   ramp for making cars go farthest? It is not necessarily the highest. You'll find that if the ramp is too
   high the cars will crash or veer off to the side.
4. Write about and/or draw a design for the ideal ramp. In other words, the children have conducted
   an experiment and made several trials. What are their conclusions? With the results of their experiment, they will know how to build a great car ramp every time.

Want to do more?

Use other materials for ramp building such as different boards or a tube. What else can the ramp be
used for? Have the children collect objects that roll or don't roll, using the ramp to test their predictions. Place the ramp on a checkered table cloth. How many squares does each car travel?

★ MUDPIES TO MAGNETS

Ticket to the Moon

4+

The moon is the most easily studied of all celestial bodies, particularly during the winter months when it rises before bedtime. A fantasy trip to the moon is the culmination of a few weeks of observing and recording its cycles.

Words to use

moon
night
full moon
half moon
three-quarter moon
crescent
cycle

Materials

photos or drawings showing the moon in different stages of its cycle
ticket box
calendar
moon tickets (small papers with a 1/2 dollar size circle on each)

What to do

1. Choose a time of year when the moon is visible early in the evening. It's fun to begin with the new moon and watch it grow. Check a calendar showing moon cycles to help in planning.
2. Show the children pictures of the moon and help them focus on the different shapes of the moon. You can even put them in order from the smaller "fingernail moon" to a full moon. "Did anyone see the moon last night? What shape is it now? Let's find out."
3. Give each of the children a moon ticket to take home with a note for their parents explaining that they are to observe the moon and fill in the circle on the moon ticket to show the moon's shape as they observe it.
4. The next day, look at the returned tickets and draw the moon on the calendar. Put the tickets in a ticket box which the children have decorated with moons and stars. As always, encourage full participation, but don't penalize those who don't return the tickets. All you actually need are a few reports each day. Continue 2 or 3 days a week until the full moon. With luck, clouds won't get in your way. As the cycle progresses talk about the various stages—new moon, half moon, etc., and refer to your pictures. Guess what the moon will look like next? Will it be bigger or smaller?
5. When you reach the full moon, cash in your tickets for an imaginary trip to the moon (see Space Helmets, page 212) or have a Full Moon Party with moon shaped snacks (round or crescent shaped cookies, cheese or toast) and moon juice (you can think that up yourself!) to drink.

Want to do more?

Share pictures of lunar landings and talk about the space program. NASA has some excellent resources. Read some poems, folk tales and stories about the moon. Sample those from around the world. Write some of your own.

★ MUDPIES TO MAGNETS

science activities

Snack and Cooking Activities

Apple Heart Pizza

3+

These hearts are for giving and for eating!

Words to use

mix
dough
shape
heart
knead
core
sprinkle
bake

Materials

2 1/4 cups flour, plus extra
1 1/4 sticks butter, room temperature
3 tablespoons plus 1 teaspoon sugar
1/4 teaspoon salt
1/4 cup cold water
3 medium-size apples
1/2 teaspoon cinnamon
oven at 400°F
spatula
cookie sheet
cutting board and knife
large and medium mixing bowl
rolling pin
apple peeler/corer

What to do

The dough

1. In a large mixing bowl, mix the flour and butter with fingers until the flour looks a little yellow. Add three tablespoons of sugar and the salt to the flour. Add the cold water and continue to blend with the hands until the dough forms a ball.

2. Spread a little flour on a cutting board. Knead the dough on the floured board for five minutes. Add more flour if needed.

FEBRUARY

snack & cooking activities

238

3. Shape the dough into a ball. Divide the ball into four equal pieces. Roll each piece with the rolling pin about one-quarter inch thick. Sprinkle flour on the dough to keep it from sticking.
4. Shape each piece into a flat heart shape by hand. Slide a spatula under the dough and place it on the cookie sheet. Do the same for the other three pieces.

The apple pizza

1. Core and peel the apples. Cut them in four quarters and then slice each quarter into about six to ten slices.
2. Place all the slices in a medium bowl. Sprinkle with one teaspoon of sugar and the cinnamon. Toss the apples, cinnamon and sugar until evenly coated.
3. Place the apple slices on each heart of dough in a pinwheel shape or any other design.
4. Bake for fifteen minutes at 400°F. When the edge is golden brown, the apple pizza hearts are ready. With adult help, remove the pizza from the oven.
5. Slide each pizza onto a plate. Eat hot, warm or cool.

Teaching tips

The dough can be rolled out ahead of time and kept covered in the refrigerator until ready to add the apples and bake.

★ PRESCHOOL ART

Red Party   3+

Children learn to make an everyday occasion festive by decorating.

Words to use

red
other color words
decorate

Materials

red napkins
red paper cups
red gelatin mix
mixing bowl and spoon
rebus chart of directions for making gelatin, optional (see page 261 for making a rebus recipe)
red construction paper

What to do

1. Early in the morning's activities, have three or four children assist you in mixing a package of gelatin.
2. After one package has been prepared, gather another group to mix a second batch.
3. Let children who have not assisted with making the gelatin decorate the tables for snacks by placing red objects from around the classroom onto red construction paper for red centerpieces.

Teaching tips

Ask the children to bring something red from home for the centerpieces for the following day. Follow the same procedure and have other colors featured on other days.

★ STORY S-T-R-E-T-C-H-E-R-S

snack & cooking activities

Small, Medium, Large Mmmmmmm!

4+

Children learn about different sizes.

Words to use

dough
roll out
small
medium
large
difference
count

Materials

several rolls of prepared cookie dough
oven
rolling pin
flour
cookie sheets
three sizes of the same shape of cookie cutter or three different cookie cutters in three
     distinct sizes

What to do

1. Have the children roll out a portion of the dough. Allow each child to cut one small, one medium and one large cookie.
2. Bake them and serve them for snack. Discuss the size differences while you eat.
3. Count how many bites it takes to eat each size.

★ THEMESTORMING

 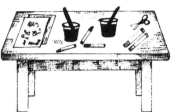

Transition Activities

Roll Call

3+

Encourages children to recognize their written names.

Words to use

name
card
recognize

Materials

index cards
markers

What to do

1. Prepare a name card for each child in the class.
2. Use the name cards to direct children for transitional activities or for playing games. Examples: "This little boy (teacher shows name) may go to the snack table." "This little girl can go outside."

★ THE INSTANT CURRICULUM

Special Spectacles

3+

Use these Special Spectacles to get children's attention. This is a positive cue that says, "I have something to tell you."

Words to use

spectacles
glasses
listen
thumb
index finger
circle

Materials

What to do

1. Using thumb and index finger on both hands, form circles.
2. Put these up next to your eyes to look like glasses as you say or sing the following.

> *I'm putting on my spectacles to see what I can see.*
> *I'm putting on my spectacles and I see*
> *(Child's name), and (child's name), and*
> *(Child's name) looking at me.*

3. As the children quiet down and make eye contact with you, say their names.

Want to do more?

Use empty glasses frames, or make some pretend glasses from pipe cleaners and plastic rings from a six pack drink holder. Encourage children to pretend to put on their "special spectacles" to look back at you. Have children put on "spectacles" before coming in from the playground to look at something they think is beautiful. Show children how to cup their hands behind their ears to make elephant ears so they can listen carefully to and remember directions. Use Special Spectacles for recall at the end of the day, for example, "Ishi, I saw your painting. Can you tell me about your picture?" "Erin, I saw you playing with blocks. What did you build?"

★ TRANSITION TIME

Masking Tape Machine   3+

Use this clean-up tool for a quick clean-up. Tape is sticky, it's fun and it will make cleaning the floor a game.

Words to use

clean up   tool
tape   sticky

Materials

masking tape

What to do

1. Give each child a piece of masking tape (approximately 6" long).
2. Show them how to wrap it around their fingers with the sticky side out.
3. Tell them they're going to be vacuum cleaners and pick up the trash on the floor with their tape.
4. Pretend to turn them "on" and make a humming sound like a vacuum cleaner.
5. When the floor is picked up, turn them "off" and have them throw their tape in the trash.

Want to do more?

Child-size brooms are perfect for sweeping floors and sidewalks, and small carpet sweepers are great for cleaning rugs. A dust buster or child-size dust pans and brushes are other useful classroom tools.

★ TRANSITION TIME

The Finger Band   3+

The Finger Band calms children down after active play, preparing them for a story or quiet time.
Fingerplays develop verbal skills, auditory memory and small motor skills.

Words to use
fingers
move

Materials
none

What to do

1. Recite the fingerplay, making the
   appropriate motions.

playing drums

> *The finger band is coming to town,*
> *(put hands behind back, then*
> *wiggle them as you bring them*
> *out in front of you)*
>
> *Coming to town, coming to town.*
> *The finger band is coming to town,*
> *So early in the morning.*
>
> *This is the way we play our drums,*
> *(pretend to play drums with your*
> *hands)*
> *Play our drums, play our drums.*
> *This is the way we play our drums,*
> *So early in the morning.*
>
> *This is the way we play our horns....(pretend to blow horns)*
> *This is the way we twirl our hats....(pretend to twirl hats)*

2. Ask children to suggest other instruments that could be in the band and make the appropriate
   motions.
3. End with the verse below.

> *The finger band is going away, (march hands behind your back as*
> *you lower your voice)*
> *Going away, going away.*
> *The finger band is going away,*
> *So early in the morning.*

4. By the time you get to the last line, your voice should be a whisper, and the children should be
   settled down and looking at you quietly.

Songs to sing

Sing The Finger Band to the tune of "The Mulberry Bush."

Did You Ever, Ever, Ever?   3+

Try this chant to extend a group activity or get children's attention. It encourages creativity in children.

Words to use

rhythm
slap
clap

Materials

What to do

1. Slap thighs and clap hands to the rhythm of this chant.

> *Did you ever, ever, ever (clap and snap to the beat)*
> *Did you ever, ever, ever*
> *See a cow take a bow?*
> *Oh, no! (put hands up in the air, then bring them down as you pretend*
>   *to laugh)*

> *Did you ever, ever, ever*
> *Did you ever, ever, ever*
> *See a dog kiss a frog?*
> *Oh, no!*

> *Did you ever, ever, ever*
> *Did you ever, ever, ever*
> *See a pig dance a jig?*
> *Oh, no!*

> *Did you ever, ever, ever*
> *Did you ever, ever, ever*
> *See a goat wear a coat?*
> *Oh, no!*

Did you ever, ever, ever
Did you ever, ever, ever
See a snake in a cake?
Oh, no!

Did you ever, ever, ever
Did you ever, ever, ever
See a moose dance with a goose?
Oh, no!

2. Encourage the children to make up their own silly verses.

Want to do more?

Make a big book to go along with the verses and let the children illustrate it.

★ TRANSITION TIME

Transition

3+

Teaches children friendship skills.

Words to use

chant
friend
hold hands
squeeze
hug

Materials

What to do

This chant is a good way to end an activity, leaving everyone feeling good.

And now it's time to stop,
But just before we do,
Everybody join your hands,
And squeeze a hug to you.

★ 500 FIVE MINUTE GAMES

Finding Colors

3+

Teaches color recognition.

Words to use

color words
flashlight

Materials

flashlight

What to do

1. Shine a flashlight on objects in the room
2. Tell the children that you are looking for something red.
3. Ask them to say, "Hooray," when the flashlight finds something red.
4. Repeat this game using different colors.
5. Try the game with shapes.

★ 500 Five Minute Games

Color Words

3+

Teaches color recognition.

Words to use

color words
identify

Materials

What to do

1. Identify things in the room that are red.
2. Walk around and say, "Tria, are you wearing red?"
3. Tria will look at her clothes and tell you if she is wearing red.
4. Encourage the children to answer in full sentences.
5. Each day try a different color.

★ 500 Five Minute Games

What's Missing?

Enhances children's observation skills.

Words to use

pictures
missing
one part

Materials

pictures of familiar objects
scissors

What to do

1. Prepare several pictures in advance of objects familiar to the children. Cut them out from magazines, catalogs and old books.
2. Cut away one part of the object, for example:
   ✓ a car missing a wheel
   ✓ a tree missing a trunk
   ✓ a spoon missing a handle
   ✓ a stuffed animal missing a tail
3. Ask the children to guess what is missing.

★ 500 FIVE MINUTE GAMES

Diddle, Diddle Dumpling

3+

This game entertains a group on a rainy day or when there are a few minutes to spare.
Children have fun guessing who took their shoe.

Words to use

shoe   circle
find   guess

Materials

What to do

1. Have the children sit in a circle.
2. Choose one child to be "John."
3. John takes off one shoe and puts it in the middle of the circle.
4. John then hides in a corner and closes his eyes.
5. Point to a child who takes "John's" shoe and hides it in his lap.

6. Say the verse below.

Diddle, diddle, dumpling,
My son, John,
Went to bed
With his trousers on.
One shoe off
And the other shoe on.
Diddle, diddle, dumpling,
My son, John.

Hey, John,
Your shoe is gone.
When you find it
You put it on.
Hey, John,
Your shoe is gone.
Find it now,
And put it on.

7. The children yell, "Wake up, John."
8. John returns to the circle and tries to guess who has his shoe.
9. He gets three guesses.
10. The person who took the shoe becomes the new "John."

★ TRANSITION TIME

Tug of Peace

3+

Never compare a child's performance to another child's to motivate her to do better. Her focus should be on setting and achieving a worthy goal, instead of doing better than someone else.

Words to use

cooperate
together
effort
group
individual
accomplish
task
encourage
move
goal
heavy
difficult

Materials

one rope about 3/4-1" thick, approximately 40-50' long
a very heavy, but moveable object (large wooden crate, piece of plywood holding a stack of bricks, small boulder, log, etc.)
gloves for children (brought from home)

What to do

1. Gather the children around you and tell them you have an activity that will require them to work together to move something heavy.
2. Tie the rope securely around the heavy object so that two equal lengths of rope remain. The object should be heavy enough that the group can successfully move it, but only with great effort. The rope should be strong enough to withstand the strain.
3. Divide the children into two equal groups and assign each group to one end of the rope. Ask them to put on their gloves. On command, both groups begin to pull the rope and try to move the object to a reasonable distance designated by the teacher. Supervise them closely for safety.
4. Do not hesitate to become involved. Shout words of encouragement and praise as the children pull. When finished, discuss the merits of cooperation to accomplish a difficult task. Point out—and let anyone who wants to, try—that no single individual can move the object alone. Only a group can do it.

Home connection

Ask parents to set up several situations in which they and their children work together to achieve a goal. For example, children and parents can lift and move a heavy box together. Parents should involve their children cooperatively even though they are capable of achieving the goal alone.

★ THE PEACEFUL CLASSROOM

Valentine, Valentine, Red and Blue 3+

Children enjoy a simple tag game with a valentine theme.

Words to use

tag
valentine
circle

Materials

one red and blue valentine

What to do

1. Have the children sit in a wide circle on the floor.
2. Pick one child to carry the red or blue valentine.
3. The child with the valentine walks around the outside of the circle while the rest of the group chants, "Valentine, valentine, red and blue, I have a valentine just for YOU!"

4. As soon as the child with the valentine hears the word "you," he puts the valentine down behind the closest child. That child picks up the valentine and tries to tag the valentine giver, who runs around the circle to the empty place and sits down. If the valentine giver is tagged, he must give the valentine away again. If the valentine giver reaches the empty space without being tagged, the child holding the valentine must now give it away.

5. The game continues until every child has had a turn to give away the valentine.

★ THE GIANT ENCYCLOPEDIA OF THEME ACTIVITIES

Valentine Game   3+

This activity promotes group cooperation and allows children to identify numbers and to exercise in place.

Words to use

heart shapes
count
beanbag
move

Materials

red construction paper
one beanbag (red and/or
    heart shaped is good)
marker
clear contact paper

What to do

1. Cut out large (dinner plate size) heart shapes. Cut an amount your children will be able to count. Write a different large number on each heart. Cover each heart with clear contact paper.

2. Explain to the children that you have hearts with numbers written on them. Hold them up, one at a time and have the class identify each number.
Next, spread the hearts face up on the floor. Do not overlap.

3. Show the beanbag to the children. Demonstrate how they can gently toss the beanbag so that it lands on one of the hearts (If the beanbag lands on the floor, let the thrower identify the heart closest to it.) Ask the child throwing the beanbag to identify the number and suggest a way of moving "in place" (i.e. jumping, twisting, bending arms, etc.).
4. Now, all together, the other children will count aloud as they do the chosen movement the number of times shown on the heart.
5. Continue the activity until each child has had a turn to toss the beanbag and suggest a way of moving.

Want to do more?

Instead of letting each child think of a movement, have a basket of small paper hearts available with different ways of moving written on them. After the child throws the beanbag and identifies the number, let him draw a small heart from the basket. The teacher can read it to the class. Continue the game as before.

★ THE GIANT ENCYCLOPEDIA OF THEME ACTIVITIES

Musical Hearts Game　　　　　　　3+

Children increase their vocabulary for Valentine's Day with "love, hug, share and heart," improve their skills in sharing and helping and enhance their ability to follow directions and rules.

Words to use

share	friends
help	music
love	stop
hug	dance
heart	directions

Materials

large roll of paper, such as butcher paper
scissors
tape
record or tape of music

What to do

1. Cut several large hearts out of roll paper. Make each one large enough that a few children can stand together on it.
2. Talk to the children about sharing with friends, helping, and ways we show we care, like hugging.
3. Explain that you are going to play a game like Musical Chairs.
4. When the music plays, the children move or dance around the hearts on the floor. When the music stops, each child finds a heart to stand on.

5. Explain that there will not be enough hearts for each child, so they will need to share with their friends. Also, sometimes it may seem like there is not enough room on the heart for any more friends, but if they try very hard, they can probably help their friends find a spot on the heart. They may have to help by holding onto their friends or "hugging" them so they won't fall off the heart.
6. Stop and start the music as in Musical Chairs.
7. After a few rounds, take one heart away each time you stop the music. Continue until only one heart remains and all the children are touching part of the heart.

Want to do more?

Have children discuss creative ways to help their friends. Some children may find unique ways to get on the heart, such as putting their hands on it or touching it with their elbow. Have children take turns controlling the music or choosing which heart to take away.

★ THE GIANT ENCYCLOPEDIA OF THEME ACTIVITIES

Heart Game   4+

Children use their large muscles and have lots of fun as they play this game—lively entertainment for Valentine's Day or any day!

Words to use

hearts
message
numbers
act out

Materials

construction paper, preferably red or pink
scissors
crayons, markers or pencils
2 dice

What to do

1. Have the children help you cut eleven large hearts out of construction paper and number them from two to twelve.
2. Write a message on the back of each heart. The message might say, for example, "make a funny face," "tell a joke," "sing a song," "pretend you are a bird (or another animal)," "cry like a baby," "say something nice to a friend," or "hug your teacher." Keep the messages on the valentine theme, or you can vary them.
3. Place all the hearts on the floor in numerical order. Make sure that the numbers are visible and the messages are face down.
4. Let the children take turns rolling the dice and turning over the heart that corresponds to that number. Read the messages and encourage children to act them out.
5. Continue until all children have had a turn.

Want to do more?

The game has many variations simply by changing the messages on the backs of the hearts. You could play it as a detective game, drawing pictures of objects in your room on the backs of the hearts and having the children find the objects and bring them to the circle. This eliminates the need for reading. Or ask everyone to do ten jumping jacks and have them feel their heartbeat.

★ THE GIANT ENCYCLOPEDIA OF THEME ACTIVITIES

Pick Up with Sticks   4+

Sometimes pairing children of a similar developmental level will be less frustrating for them than the results of random assignments or letting children choose their own partners.

Words to use

cooperate
partner
volunteer
work together
group
encourage
opportunity

Materials

two slender lengths of wood, about
    2' long and about 1" x 2"
a balloon, nerf ball, tennis ball, golf
    ball or similar substitutes
a container no higher than 1' to hold
    the balls (a large grocery bag, cut
    to about 6" in height would work)

What to do

1. Set the balloon and the container next to each other in the center of the circle. Tell the children you would like to see if they can cooperate with a partner to put the balloon into the bag. When one child volunteers to try, select a partner for him.
2. Give each child one of the wood sticks. Tell them the object of the game is for them to work together, to cooperate, to pick up the balloon with their sticks and place it in to the bag. Encourage the rest of the group to cheer them on.
3. If they succeed with the balloon, continue with the nerf ball, then the tennis ball, and finally, the golf ball. If the balloon is too difficult, take turns being each child's partner, coaching them as you proceed. Step back and let them try as partners once again. Be generous with your words of encouragement as they work together.
4. When they are through, give others an opportunity to try as well.

Want to do more?

Vary the size, shape and firmness of the objects to be picked up. Vary the lengths and shape of the sticks. Long dowel rods are the most difficult to handle. Make the task difficult enough to provide a challenge, but not so difficult as to be unnecessarily frustrating.

Home connection

Parents and children can work together on a similar task at home. Suggest a simple activity like picking up a small crumpled piece of paper with two butter knives. For a more exciting challenge, try picking up a boiled egg.

★ THE PEACEFUL CLASSROOM

Are You Sick? 4+

A relatively complex act like caretaking can be broken down into its fundamental components. In this activity, provide simple, easily understood explanations of the causes and consequences of being sick or hurt. Avoid using the word "bug" to refer to bacteria or viruses. Describe and discuss symptoms of illness like sore throat, cough, fever, upset stomach. Provide factual reassurance to children who are frightened about an illness or accident.

Words to use

sick
gentle
yucky feelings
care

Materials

blanket
pillow
washcloth
bowl with a small amount of warm water

What to do

1. Ask the children if they have ever been sick. Take a few moments to discuss times when they were ill.
2. Introduce the activity with the following story:

> *Once upon a time in Butterberry Hill, Amy became very sick. Her mommy brought her a blanket and pillow so she could lay down. Because Amy was sick, her temperature went up, and she became very hot. Her mommy and daddy took a damp washcloth and gently washed her face to make her feel cooler. After two days of rest and loving care, Amy felt better and could go to school once again. The End.*

3. Tell the children that you have an activity in which they will pretend to care for someone who is sick. Ask for a volunteer to pretend to be sick. Ask the volunteer to go to the center of the circle and lie down on his back. Ask him to point to someone who can help him.
4. Ask the helper to put the pillow under the "sick" child's head and to cover him with a blanket. Then set the bowl and washcloth near the sick child's head. Ask him to close his eyes and then have the helper gently sponge his forehead and cheeks with the washcloth dipped in warm water.
5. Ask for another volunteer to be the pretend sick person and continue with other rounds of gentle caretaking.

Want to do more?

You can set up a make-believe "hospital" in the dress-up area where two or three children pretend to be ill.

Home connection

Parents can ask children to place a damp washcloth on their forehead when they have a headache or need to relax.

★ THE PEACEFUL CLASSROOM

Night Flying 5+

For this activity, the children must understand such movement commands as move left, move right, move forward, turn around and stop. Be sure the room is entirely free of clutter. Allow children to remove the blindfolds at any time. If there is another adult in the classroom, demonstrate the activity before the children begin.

Words to use

cooperation
guide
rescue
blindfold
right
left
directions
partner

Materials

blindfold
small blanket

What to do

1. Begin the activity with the following story:

> *Once upon a time near Butterberry Hill, a small airplane was trying to land at the airport. But the night was dark, and the lights on the runway were not working. Amy's dad was in the control tower. He could see the plane on his radar, so he got on the radio and told the pilot what direction to fly in order to land on the runway. The people on the plane were very happy when they arrived safely. The End.*

2. Tell the children you have a game for them to play about flying at night. One person will be like Amy's dad, guiding another person who is blindfolded and pretends to be the airplane. The helper guides the airplane from one side of the room to a small blanket on the other side. The helper guides only by telling the airplane where to go.
3. The children must be sufficiently mature to understand how to move to the right and to the left. Ask the children to stand and gather in a group behind you. Lead them through the directions with their eyes open. Move to the left, stop, move to the right, stop, turn around. Say the directions out loud as you move. Invite one child to stand in front of the group and give them directions.
4. Spread a small blanket on one side of the room. This is the airport. Take out a blindfold and ask if anyone would like to try the activity with a partner. The partners will have to decide between them who will be the guide and who will be the airplane.
5. Put the blindfold on the airplane. When ready, the guide can begin directing the airplane to the airport. He can accompany the airplane but should not physically direct the partner. The teacher should remain close by to ensure safety.
6. Upon arriving at the blanket, the guide may tell the airplane to sit down and remove the blindfold.
7. Repeat the activity, switching roles.

Want to do more?

Children who have difficulty giving verbal directions can stand behind their partners and gently guide them toward the goal, telling them when they arrive. Children who are proficient in this activity can try "Drop in the Bucket." To increase difficulty, try having more than one airplane or setting a timer (for a few minutes) to indicate when the airplane runs out of fuel. To decrease difficulty, try the activity without blindfolds. Whisper to the guide an object or location for the airplane to fly to. The guide then directs the airplane without specifically mentioning the goal.

Book to read

The Crab Prince retold and illustrated by Christopher Manson

★ THE PEACEFUL CLASSROOM

Books

The Car Trip by Helen Oxenbury
Flying by Donald Crews
Freight Train by Donald Crews
Goodnight Moon by Margaret Wise Brown
Grandfather Twilight by Barbara Berger
The Great Blueness and Other Predicaments by Arnold Lobel
Little Blue and Little Yellow by Leo Lionni
The Little Engine That Could by Watty Piper
Mary Wore Her Red Dress and Henry Wore His Green Sneakers by Merle Peek
The Mixed Up Chameleon by Eric Carle
Moon Song by Mildred Meigs
Move Over, Twerp by Martha Alexander
Night in the Country by Cynthia Rylant
No Jumping on the Bed! by Tedd Arnold
The Polar Express by Chris Van Allsburg
Sky All Around by Anna Grossnickle Hines
Train Leaves the Station by Eve Merriam
The Train to Lulu's by Elizabeth Fitzgerald Howard
Trains by Gail Gibbons
Truck Song by Diane Siebert
The Wheels on the Bus by Maryann Kovalski
Wheels on the Bus by Raffi
The Wheels on the Bus by Paul Zelinsky
Who Said Red? by Mary Serfozo
Why the Sun and Moon Live in the Sky by Elphinstone Dayrell
A Witch Got on at Paddington Station by Dyan Sheldon

Records, Tapes and CDs

Beall, Pamela Conn and Susan Hagen Nipp. "Down by the Station" from *Wee Sing Sing-Alongs*. Price Stern Sloan, 1990.

Beall, Pamela Conn and Susan Hagen Nipp. "Twinkle, Twinkle, Little Star" from *Wee Sing Children's Songs and Fingerplays*. Price Stern Sloan, 1979.

Hammett, Carol Totsky and Elaine Bueffel. "Wheels on the Bus" from *Toddlers on Parade*. Kimbo.

Jenkins, Ella. "The Jolly Bus Line" and "I Love to Ride the Bus" from *This-A-Way and That-A-Way*. Folkways, 1973.

Moore, Thomas. "The Bus Driver" and "Twinkle, Twinkle, Little Star" from *Singing, Moving and Learning*. Thomas Moore Records.

Palmer, Hap. "This Is a Song About Colors" from *Learning Basic Skills Through Music: Volume 1*. Activity Records, 1969.

Scelsa, Greg and Steve Millang. "Believe in Yourself" from *Kidding Around with Greg and Steve*. Youngheart Records, 1985.

Sharon, Lois and Bram. "Pufferbellies" from *One, Two, Three, Four, Live!* Elephant Records, 1982.

Sharon, Lois and Bram. "Starlight" from *One Elephant, Deux Elephants*. Elephant, 1978.

Sharon, Lois and Bram. "Train Is A-Comin" from *Singing 'n Swinging*. Elephant Records, 1980.

Color Me a Rainbow. Melody House.

FEBRUARY

Winter Activities
Listed by Source

500 Five Minute Games

December—Can You Name _____ ?; Here Come the Robots; Jump Three Times; The Mystery Food; Mystery Music; Ten Little Reindeer; Twinkle, Twinkle; Two Fine Gentlemen

January—C-C-C-C-Cold; Catch the Falling Snow; Hungry Bunny; Interesting Talk; Listen to the Snow; Oh, Doctor Jane; Sleigh Ride; The Snowman; Storytelling Together; Word Sharing

February—Color Words; Finding Colors; Groundhog; Let's Travel; Pussy Willow; Transition; What's Missing?; Wheels on the Bus

The Complete Learning Center Book

December—Postcards; Post Office with Mail Boxes; Toy Puppets; Toy Puzzles; Toy Workshop Center; Writing Center

January—Ambulance for Emergency Care; Doctor's Office/Hospital Center; Flannel Board Stories; The Librarian; Library Center; Medical Charting

February—Baskets for Groceries; The Dark Place; Flashlights; Grocery Store Center; Nighttime Center

Earthways

December—Pine Cone Bird Feeders; Pine Cone Fire Starters; Pomander Balls; Star Windows: Tissue Paper Transparencies; Tissue Paper Dolls; Wooden Candleholders; Yarn Dolls

January—Finger Knitting; Snow Scenes

February—Valentine Hearts; Valentine Mice; Valentine Swans

The GIANT Encyclopedia of Circle Time and Group Activities

December—Dreidel Game and Activities; Jingle Bell Blanket; Little Drummer Girls and Boys; Musical Christmas Present Surprise; Shining Stars

January—Five Little Snowmen Fat; Let's Go Ice Skating; Making Soft Pretzels; Popping Popcorn; Snowfolks; Snowman, Snowman; What Can You Do in Winter Time?

February—Airplane Song and Activities; Color Magic; How Did You Get to School Today?; Hurry, Hurry, Fire Truck; My Favorite Color Chart; Transportation; Who Is Wearing Red Today?

The GIANT Encyclopedia of Theme Activities

December—Christmas Egg Carton Tree; Glittering Pine Cones; Five Little Candy Canes; Flannel Board Story Box; Light the Kwanzaa Candles

January—Balancing Beanbags; Color the Movement; Ice Castles; Making Horns; Mitten Match; Snowflakes

February—An Owl Valentine; Constructing a Car; Heart Game; How Do I Get There?; Ladybug's Family; Musical Hearts Game; Road, Sky or Water; Tire Prints; Valentine Game; Valentine, Valentine, Red and Blue

Hug a Tree

December—Take a Bird to Lunch

January—How Deep Is Your Snow Drift?; Snowjob; Tin Can Ice Cream

The Instant Curriculum

December—Christmas Tree Decorating; Circles to Music; Crescendo; Freckles and Stripes

January—Bottle Maracas; Drums and Sticks; What Is It?; Winter Pictures

February—Air Pushers; Box Cars and Boats; Broken Names; Experience Charts; Funny Funny Papers; Giants and Elves; Listening for the Horses; Name Game; Preschool Limbo; Raisin Elevators; Roll Call; Ship Ahoy; Sing and Listen; Torn Paper Silhouettes; Twin Tunes; Variations on Old Time Favorites

The Learning Circle

January—Cold Talk; Winter Wind

February—Sorting

More Mudpies to Magnets

December—Hot Bubble Fliers; How Fast Does Your Crystal Grow?

January—The Big Melt Down

February—School Map Puzzle

More Story S-t-r-e-t-c-h-e-r-s

December—Decorating Windows with Snowflakes; Decorating with Food Coloring; Packing for Our Visit; Replicating Patterns with Blocks; Weather Vanes; Writing about Our Travel Adventures

January—Horizontal Bar Graphs of Birds at Our Winter Feeder; How Many Objects Fit on the Paper?; Movement Clues to Solve Riddles

February—Favorite Color Day; Our Favorite Bedtime Books; Putting Children to Bed; Writing a Nighttime Walking Adventure

Mudpies to Magnets

December—Good and Juicy; Orange You Glad They're Not All Alike?

January—Cave in a Box; Grow a Rock; Mushy, Slushy, Melty Snow; Thermometer Play

February—The Great Air Machine Race; Rampin' It; Space Helmets; Ticket to the Moon

One Potato, Two Potato, Three Potato, Four

December—Little Jack Horner; Star Light, Star Bright; Twinkle, Twinkle

January—Frosty Weather, Snowy Weather; The North Wind Doth Blow; Polly, Put the Kettle On; Sally Go 'Round the Sun; Snow, Snow, Fly Away; This Is a Snowman As Round As a Ball

February—Deedle, Deedle Dumpling; Engine, Engine Number Nine; Hey, Diddle, Diddle; Wee Willie Winkie

The Outside Play and Learning Book

January—Bird Pudding; Don't Move — Help Is on the Way; Follow My Tracks; Footprints in the Snow; Fox and Geese Game; Hide and Seek Tracking; Snow Drawings and Prints; Spray Painting Designs in Snow

February—Body Part Matching; Fill'er Up and Fix'er Up!; Fire!; Obstacle Course; Treasure Hunt

The Peaceful Classroom

December—Partner Kickball; Rubber Band; Taste Helpers; Wonder Wands

January—Cookie Machine; Cooperative Towers; Crossing the Bridge; My Friend; Night Train; The Star Seat; Still Water

February—Are You Sick?; Night Flying; Pick Up with Sticks; Tug of Peace; Won or Two

Preschool Art

December—Bread Sculptures; Fabric Transfer; Insole Stamps; Light Holes; Stained Glass Melt; String Ornaments; Window Paintings

January—Paste Batik; Salt Figurines; Snow Paint; Snowy Etching; Stuffed Stuff

February—Apple Heart Pizza; Heart a L'art; Heart Flutters; Lace Rubbing;Tissue Contact

Story S-t-r-e-t-c-h-e-r-s

December—Imaginary Dancing; Magnetic Rice; Pilots and Flight Attendants; Reaching, Stretching, Growing, Knowing

January—Ice Skater's Waltz; Mitten, Mitten, Who Has the Mitten?; Musical I Spy; Relaxing to Music; Snowmen and Snowwomen Cookies; Snowy Mashed Potatoes; Sweet Honey

February—Counting Cars, Vans, Trucks, Buses; Red Party; Truck Sounds

ThemeStorming

December—Mirror Skating; String Kabobs
January—Blizzards; Hide the Mitten; Mitten Safari
February—Small, Medium, Large Mmmmmm!

Transition Time

December—Art Parade; Coat Hanger Critter; Follow the Flashlight; Lollipops; Make a Lap; The Quiet Touch

January—Book Buddies; Four Corners; Hot Potato; I'll Find a Friend; Little Mouse; Puppet Pals and Inspectors; Snowmen; The Snap Rap; A Story Box; Teeny Tiny Friends

February—Did You Ever, Ever, Ever?; Diddle, Diddle Dumpling; The Finger Band; Five Red Valentines; Masking Tape Machine; Special Spectacles

Where Is Thumbkin?

December—Balancing and Spinning; Christmas Is Coming; Christmas Potpourri; Counting Bags; Eight; Latkes; Hanukkah Song; Homemade Sleigh; Jingle Bells; Making Dreidels; Menorah Flannel Pieces; My Dreidel; Mystery Package; Paper Chains; Sponge Trees; Sugar Cookies; Tree Seriation; We Wish You a Merry Christmas; Wrapping Presents

January—Big and Little Mittens; The Feely Box; Footprint Concentration; The Fox; Graphing; Ice Painting; Making Peanut Butter; Marvelous Mittens; The Mulberry Bush; Patterns; Peanut Butter; Peanut Collage; Recipe Collection; The Three Little Kittens; Where Is Thumbkin?

February—Are You Sleeping?; Color Song; Down by the Station; New Words; Pretend Bus; Shoe Box Train; Sorting Stars (formerly Sorting); Spool Painting; Star Designs; Star Wishes; Train Sequence; Twinkle, Twinkle, Little Star; Vehicles; The Wheels on the Bus

Sample Rebus Chart
Directions for Making Muffins

1. Preheat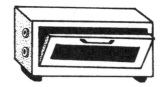

2. Place in

3. Empty into

4. Add 1 ⬭ and ½ 🥛 water

5. Stir 🥣

6. Pour into

7. Bake in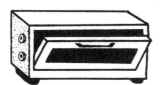

8. Serve and

Steps in Binding a Book

  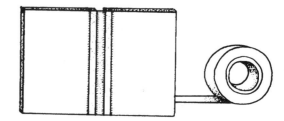

1. Cut two pieces of heavy cardboard slightly larger than the pages of the book.

2. With wide masking tape, tape the two pieces of cardboard together with ½-inch space between.

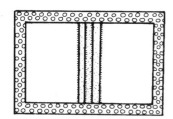  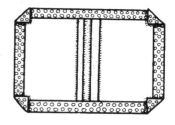

3. Cut outside cover 1½ inches larger than the cardboard and stick to cardboard (use thinned white glue if cover material is not self-adhesive.)

4. Fold corners over first, then the sides.

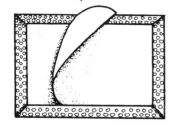 

5. Measure and cut inside cover material and apply as shown.

6. Place stapled pages of the book in the center of the cover. Secure with two strips of inside cover material, one at the front of the book and the other at the back.

Winter Indexes

Index of Terms

Children's Book Index

Recommended Titles

The GIANT Encyclopedia of Theme Activities For Children 2 to 5

Over 600 Favorite Activities
Created by Teachers for Teachers

Edited by Kathy Charner

The result of a nationwide contest, this book offers 48 themes and clear descriptions of 600 ready-to-use teacher-developed activities. From the alphabet and art to winter and zoo, you will find themes for every season and every day of the year. All activities require minimum preparation and have been proven successful in the classroom. This book has a special strengthened binding, allowing it to lie flat on a table. An ideal resource for a busy teacher. 512 pages. © 1993.

ISBN-13: 978-0-87659-166-6
Gryphon House
19216
Paperback

Count on Math

Activities for Small Hands and Lively Minds

Pam Schiller and Lynne Peterson

Math makes sense to children when they learn it using the activities in **Count on Math**. Packed with over 450 hands-on activities, each chapter introduces a math concept with the definition of the concept, links to other math concepts, suggestions for success, a list of key words, and a circle time story. Numerous child-and teacher-initiated activities use everyday materials. each chapter ends with suggestions to evaluate children's learning and a newsletter to copy and send home. 271 pages. © 1997.

ISBN-13: 978-0-87659-188-8
Gryphon House
18251
Paperback

*Available at your favorite bookstore,
school supply store or order from Gryphon House®*